PROMISE
OR PERIL

The Black College Student in America

BY THE SAME AUTHOR: *The Betrayal*

PROMISE
OR PERIL

The Black College Student in America

William R. Corson

W · W · NORTON & COMPANY · INC · NEW YORK

SBN 393 05405 5

FIRST EDITION

Copyright © 1970 by William R. Corson. All rights reserved. Published simultaneously in Canada by George J. McLeod Limited, Toronto. *Library of Congress Catalog Card No. 78-90983.* Printed in the United States of America.

1 2 3 4 5 6 7 8 9 0

To the memory of Michael C. Wunsch, Captain,
U.S. Marine Corps, killed in action, July 28, 1969,
who believed in the worth of all men

CONTENTS

7

PREFACE

THIS BOOK MAY BE LIKENED TO a sonar system reporting sounds which, although still below the threshold of our hearing, are already changing the structure and meaning of race-related problems in our society. The sounds are the voices of the black college students as they express their expectations, aspirations, plans, and fears. The unifying theme of this book is the proposition that the black college students' future is imperiled on the one hand by institutional white racism and on the other by the possibility of their participation in a revolution led by black revolutionaries who have given up all hope for peace and freedom between the races in America.

I have tried to look at the dimensions of the fears, the perceptions, the values, the opportunities, and the goals of the black college students. I take a broad view—not only of the alternatives and their effect on black students but also of their effect on the totality of American society. Without the students, black extremists cannot mount their revolution; with them they may be able to. Without the help of black college students, white and black moderates will not be able to resolve the racial conflicts which divide our nation. The black college student, then, is the key variable. The number of black people committed to revolution is small, their organizations fragmented, their ideology simply rule or ruin. Yet if they succeed in recruiting the black college generation they can multiply their numbers, centralize their organization, and refine and effectively communicate their ideologies. Revolution then will become possible.

I have examined the pressures that may cause black college students to abandon their hopes of fulfilling themselves within our present American society and turn instead to the open-ended violence of a race war, and I have outlined the techniques available for black revolution. Finally, some ways are suggested to reach a more peaceful tomorrow.

My debt to the students at Howard University, without whom this book never could have been written, is very great. This book is, at best, only a partial repayment for the honesty and candor with which they "taught" their teacher. My motive in writing this book has been my conviction that the views of the black students must be brought to a wider audience. What they are saying is the promise and peril of American society, and their voices are not strident or desperate. My intention is not to speak "for" the black college students, but rather to transmit their personal wisdom and their dreams for a better America, which they are willing to share with those who care to listen. They are, of course, absolved from responsibility for any errors made by me in trying to report their views. Their detailed criticisms and comments, always made in a spirit of honest give and take, improved the manuscript's content substantially. But even more important to me has been the stimulation of daily contact with them as a teacher, counselor, and friend.

Finally, among the many people who influence a person, one's wife has a predominant position. It is she who is largely responsible for the environment in which he works. Mine has come close to the ideal, so all shortcomings of this work are mine alone.

WILLIAM R. CORSON

Chevy Chase, Maryland
November 1969

PROMISE
OR PERIL

The Black College Student in America

———————————————

ONE

Introduction

IN THE CACOPHONY of our racial problems if there is one voice we should listen to it is that of the black college student. In writing this book I have listened to that voice, in trying to find an answer to the questions "What are the black students *really* saying?" and "Where do they stand in relation to a potential black revolution?"

The answers are both encouraging and alarming. Encouraging because the black college student is inclined to reject revolution and violent confrontation as the means to reach his place in society, alarming because he is being increasingly subjected by the black activists and potential revolutionaries to a wide variety of pressures that could possibly serve to radicalize him anyway.* There is no assurance that the black student will continue to reject revolution; he is skeptical of American society's ability and pessimistic about its willingness to deliver on past promises made to Negroes. If his skepticism becomes conviction and his pessimism becomes desperation, revolution might well seem to be a plausible alternative.

It was an extended conversation with the late Bernard Fall

* Throughout this book "militancy" refers to the almost universal black impatience with the rate of social change and the elimination of racism, "activist" to an individual or organization committed to protest and disruptive action to achieve his ends, and "revolutionary" to an individual or organization that has clearly demonstrated a definite potential for violent revolutionary activity.

in South Vietnam about the possibility of a black revolution in
the United States that led me, first, to an examination of the attitudes of the Negro Marines under my command in the Marine
Corps's Combined Action Program and then to take a teaching
position at Howard University in Washington. Fall, who at the
time of his death was on leave from his post as Professor of International Relations at Howard, had come to Vietnam to do research for a new book about the U.S. role in the Vietnam War.
In connection with his research, he came to the III Marine Am-
phibious Force headquarters on the morning of February 21,
1967, to discuss the Combined Action Program with me.

Our conversation ranged from the problems of pacification
to the higher conduct of the war, but Fall kept returning to his
theory of a parallel between the Vietnamese revolutionary experience and the American racial situation. Because he was almost
completely obsessed with the concept that Vietnam is a perfect
illustration of the West's inability to engage in counterrevolutionary action, I tended to discount the completeness of his
Vietnamese parallel. He admitted that the historical analogue of
Vietnam with the United States was not complete, but he was
adamant on one point—that the current racial turbulence in the
United States was not just one more chapter in the history of
our race relations, but represented a significant departure from
the previous evolutionary process to one of real revolution.
When I pressed him on the point, he said, "I know I am being
unscientific. I could argue the point on the basis that many of
the same things affecting the American Negro, such as the lack
of upward social mobility, inferior education, and economic exploitation, were responsible for turning the Viet Cong into a viable revolutionary force—but it's more than that. There is a qual-
itative change underway which is not quantifiable, but which,
nonetheless, is most real." Then he laughed and added, "I
shouldn't have to explain it to you—your nose for revolution is
better than mine." Whether my nose for revolution was better
than Bernard Fall's is beside the point, but he was right—the
"smell" of revolution is no less real than the smell of a decaying
corpse. It is just that we are better able to identify the latter
than the former.

Because Fall had been teaching at Howard University,

where 93 per cent of the student body is black, I suggested that he was reflecting the attitudes and opinions of his students. He confirmed this and added that although there was as yet no Condorcet among the black students, there were many who were willing to play the role of Robespierre in an American version of the French Revolution's Reign of Terror.*

When we parted—he to meet his death in less than an hour from a Viet Cong mine while riding in a Marine Corps jeep along the "Street Without Joy"—he left me with a final disquieting thought: "Bill, you're involved in the wrong counterrevolution. It's too late for Vietnam—and perhaps too late for America. If any 'hearts and minds' really can and should be won they are black and they are in the United States." Death has a way of etching a man's last remarks into one's conscience and memory.

Between the time of Bernard Fall's death in February 1967 and my departure from Vietnam in September I was often forced to recall his words about racial violence and revolution in America. It seemed that the incompetence and intransigence of the Government of South Vietnam in dealing with political, social, economic, religious, and racial discrimination, which provided the Viet Cong with the fuel they needed to drive their revolutionary engine, was being reflected in the news from the United States. During this period the attitudes of Negro Marines who were serving in Combined Action Platoons in native hamlets were very revealing because they showed, among other things, that they could see a similarity between the problems of the Vietnamese peasant and those of the black poor in the United States.

Since the Negro Marines were so sensitive to the Vietnamese peasants' problems we made a conscious effort to recruit a high proportion of Negroes into the program. This was a calculated risk because, in spite of a vast public relations effort on the part of the military establishment to portray the racial har-

* The reference to Condorcet, who as one of the intellectual leaders of the French Revolution provided the necessary justification to the bourgeois class to support the revolution's violence, is most appropriate because among the black activists such as Cleaver, Brown, and Newton there is not one who has been able to fully capture the black college student's imagination.

mony between blacks and whites during combat operations, racial hostility among American servicemen is never far from the surface in Vietnam, and we didn't want to create a "critical black mass" in the CAPs. This possibility was lessened somewhat by screening both the white and black volunteers for the program to remove the military's equivalent of a racist—that is, a "gook hater"—even though the risk was not totally eliminated. But the gamble was well worth the risk, for by both word and deed the Negro Marines did a monumental job, and not once did they betray the trust conferred on them by the peasants. Most of these black Marines, who only a year or so previously had been part of the "Negro problem" in the United States, positively demonstrated the true meaning of empathy. In the interaction with the Vietnamese people they acquired a dignity and purpose which for the most part had been denied them in American society.

In an attempt to understand what the CAP Marines felt about living among the Vietnamese peasants we conducted an in-depth study of their attitudes. The results showed that both black and white Marines recognized in the peasants a group of people who through no fault of their own were systematically oppressed by every institution in Vietnam except their own families and the self-ordered unofficial hamlet hierarchy, and they were easily persuaded—largely by themselves—to stand on the side of the people against the government's pervasive institutional repression. However, the Negro Marines' perception extended to a genuine personal identification with the peasants. Time after time we were amazed at how the Negro Marines knew, almost instinctively, what should and could be done to improve the lot of the people in a specific hamlet.

There is no need to unduly glamorize or make heroic the actions of the CAP Marines, both black and white, in meeting people on common ground. They did it, and their actions speak for themselves. But do these actions have any meaning outside of Vietnam? I think they do, for they illustrate that the root of dissension is the struggle of the individual to discover, affirm, and maintain his personal identity in the face of the challenges posed by a hostile environment. This is the personal battle the Negro CAP Marines were able to fight for the first time in their lives on a color-blind battlefield against all that threatened or appeared to threaten their sense of self. They won that fight, and an understanding of their struggle has meaning for the purpose of this book. The Negro CAP Marines learned in the crucible of war that the *I* cannot survive without a *thou*. To relate one's personal dialectic with life to others is tremendously difficult, and in the process each Negro Marine came to understand that the Negro problem was also his problem. This was the main thing I learned from my association with these young men. Given a responsibility for others they acquired, on the one hand, a personal sense of identity and, on the other, an appreciation of the worth of group solidarity. Together, these two factors are a powerful social force to prevent discrimination of any kind.

One particularly perceptive Negro corporal expressed this abstraction and its implications very succinctly when he told me: "What I have learned here is worth all the dying because I know now, for sure, that I am a man and nowhere, never again, am I going to let any man put his foot on my neck or on my people's neck." In varying degrees each of the Negroes expressed the same sentiments. There wasn't a corresponding commitment to any organizational movement as the means to insure their survival or well-being, but neither was there an outright rejection of any group, no matter how extreme. Several of the black Marines showed me the "black power" literature that finds its way unerringly to Vietnam in substantial quantity. The material was carefully chosen. It was not subversive per se, nor was it designed to recruit the Negro servicemen—in advance—into any organization; it was more a "soft sell" pitch to remind black servicemen of what was going on at home among his people and to point out the opinion voiced by Benjamin Franklin two centuries ago: "We shall all hang together, or assuredly we shall all hang separately." The Marines' reaction to this literature was consistent. They believed that as a result of their accomplishments in Vietnam they would be able to make it back in the States, and if they ran into trouble once they were out of the service, *then* they would decide whether to join the movement.

In the winter and spring of 1967, without notable exception, the black Marines were skeptical but they were not unduly pessimistic. However, by the summer of 1967, as the events sur-

rounding domestic racial violence evolved, they had shifted
from a mood of skepticism to one of defiant resignation—that is,
almost a belief in the inevitability of a physical confrontation
between themselves and the white establishment.

I have dwelt at some length on the attitudes of the black
CAP Marines toward their position in a post-Vietnam War
America because their "show me" attitude represented in micro-
cosm the response of those blacks who were able to stand somewhat outside the arena of racial confrontation and defer taking
an active stand on one side or the other. In this sense, in 1967,
the Negro CAP Marine and the black college student were in
similar positions. However, since that time the situation has
changed markedly for the black college student, and for members of all other hitherto uncommitted groups, because they
have been subjected to ever-increasing pressures to get off of
the morally neutral seventh rung of hell.

In retrospect, although black America's skepticism seems to
have been a self-fulfilling prophecy, the significance of 1967's racial violence was misperceived by white America not only because of a blindly naïve faith in the inevitability of an evolutionary improvement in race relations, but also because white
America wanted to misperceive the reality. The Great Society's
laws were on the books, the leaders of the civil rights movement
were preaching nonviolence, and America was in the midst of
an economic boom. Yet the Great Society's "War on Poverty"
was—like the War in Vietnam—stalemated; such upcoming
black leaders as H. Rap Brown, Huey Newton, Stokely Carmichael, and Eldridge Cleaver discarded Martin Luther King's
New Testament-inspired call for brotherly love in favor of the
Old Testament's command of an eye for an eye, a tooth for a
tooth; and the economic boom was less than real as prices for
all things continued to rise.

If 1967 may be likened to the prologue of America's own
Greek tragedy, then the events of 1968 and 1969 constitute the
first act of the most significant revolution of the twentieth century.

In the pellmell rush of political events in 1968, the gradual

expansion of organized black revolutionary militancy was somewhat obscured by the widespread, largely spontaneous violence
following the assassination of Martin Luther King, Jr., which
may or may not have had genuine revolutionary significance.
What is clear is that regardless of the course of future racial violence in the United States, never again will the relations between black and white be the same. The opportunities of the
past to solve racial problems on the basis of mutual trust between blacks and whites, as advocated by Dr. King, are gone
forever. We have fewer options now because in the days following Dr. King's death the protective mask worn by many American Negroes was ripped away to show clearly, for the first time,
the extent of their rage and hatred, and once these emotions had
been sprung out of Pandora's box there was no way or no one
who could easily put them back. The murder of Robert F. Kennedy on June 5, 1968, was the capstone to black despondency
and despair. The death of popular leaders always produces a social trauma, but it is usually temporary unless those leaders
were identified closely with a socially alienated group. Both
Martin Luther King and Robert Kennedy were, and it took their
deaths to show the depth of social alienation among all members of the black community. With the death of Senator Kennedy the blacks lost the last white man in a position of leadership in whom they had any confidence.

The signals of genuine deep-seated social alienation are
never especially clear in the incipient stages of revolution because they are brief and emitted in a random fashion. However,
if one is attuned to the signals' characteristics it is possible to
recognize them and distinguish their intensity. In this regard, a
friend in the Justice Department with whom I shared Bernard
Fall's apprehensions about a black revolution in the United
States suggested that if Howard University was not the site of a
revolutionary transmitter, it was at least serving as a revolutionary incubator. At the time of our conversation—December
1967—Howard seemed to be a most unlikely candidate as a revolutionary incubator because of Congress' close rein on its
finances and its conservative, almost apolitical reputation. We
discussed the point in some detail and my friend finally sug-

gested that I check it for myself, because in matters of revolution information once or twice removed from the source is often conflicting or misleading.

Thus I applied for a position as a professor of economics at Howard University because I felt that the attitudes of the students in the field of economics would reflect more clearly the dilemma of those who were not yet committed to a revolutionary course of action. During my interviews about the faculty position in early January 1968 I was inclined to dismiss the idea that Howard University was anything more than a university struggling to live within its means and provide a reasonable education for black students. However, between the time I applied for an appointment to the faculty and my acceptance, the roof caved in on the university administration and its faculty leaders. On the morning of March 1, 1968, several hundred students seized a number of the university buildings and presented their demands for change to the administration authorities.

This action was the first of its kind on a college campus in the United States and in a very significant way it was different from all succeeding student uprisings, although its unique features were overlooked in the months that followed; it was assumed to be merely a forerunner to the seize, confront, and provoke incidents staged by the Students for a Democratic Society at Columbia and other universities later in 1968. The Howard takeover was characterized by strict organization and discipline, which are usually absent in student-administration confrontations and which are certainly not an automatic by-product of social protest, because they require hard work and a clear understanding of the objectives sought. The students' prime objective in the Howard seizure was a substantial improvement in the quality of their education, and their demands were carefully worked out in advance of the takeover.

The entire operation was almost a textbook model of an exercise in social reform. The seizure was swift and efficient; there was no damage to any university property throughout the five or six days of occupation; the switchboard was manned and operated; internal discipline was maintained by the students themselves; food was brought in on a regular schedule. The students left the door open for dialogue and discussion with the university authorities, and when the administration indicated its willingness to explore with them what could be done to meet their demands, the seizure was called off as quickly as it had been launched. The students apparently believed that the university would work with them to solve the problems in good faith, but —as the people who hired me made clear—this was not to be the case.

Shortly after Howard's administration had "accepted for further study" the striking students' demands, I formally accepted the previously tendered faculty appointment. At this time one fact was obvious: the university's administration and faculty leadership had become literally petrified in the face of "black student power," so petrified that they revealed to me—a newcomer in their midst—that they believed the student takeover had been part of a sinister Communist conspiracy. They said that professors who were secret Communist agents had "come out of the woodwork" to support the students, that the student demands were totally unreasonable (the term nonnegotiable was not yet in vogue) and based on a Marxist view of shared authority in running a university, and that nonstudents were using Howard as a center for the distribution of "black power" literature to other Negro colleges. In short, the only "influence" they could detect in the seizure was "Communist conspiracy."

Another revealing aspect of the potentially revolutionary situation at Howard was the students' reaction to the assassination of Martin Luther King. Although the civil disorder following the killing was widespread and seemingly spontaneous throughout the country—and especially in Washington—and although Howard straddles one of the ghetto corridors in Washington in which there was extensive damage during the outbursts, the overwhelming majority of Howard's students took no part in the rioting, and student activist leaders went to great lengths to keep the campus "cool." There are several possible explanations for the students' behavior.

Either they were more "responsible" than the rioters, their grief over Dr. King's death overcame any tendency they might have had to run with the riotous herd, or there was a conscious design on the part of the activist student leaders to avoid a punitive reaction from the police and troops against them, because to riot—at that time—was not a part of their basic strategy. Probably all three reasons were contributory, but the third one is especially revealing in a revolutionary context because it reflects a refusal to confront the power structure at a time and place outside the activists' span of effective control.

Although it cannot be proved that this was one of the reasons the students did not participate in the "spontaneous riots" following Dr. King's murder, it should not be dismissed. For if it did mark the beginning of a change in the form of violent black protest to more strategic acts of violence and a shift from massive ghetto rioting to urban guerrilla warfare, then the roots of black revolutionary violence may go far deeper than can be determined from an analysis of single, apparently random acts of violence.°

Another insight into where the student activist at Howard University stood in relation to the white power structure is revealed in a picture that appeared in the *Washington Post* on April 6, 1968. It showed six or seven students, some clad in dashikis, lowering the American flag in front of the main dormitory and preparing to replace it with the Black Liberation Front's flag. It was, symbolically, a defiant rejection of the assimilationist view of race relations in the United States. Although this may be more mildly interpreted as just another manifestation of student pique and impatience, to do so is to be deceived about the depth and intensity of the black commitment to unconditional freedom.

Before we can resolve the question of whether the black students are crying out for honesty and justice or putting white America on notice that they no longer have any hope that

---

° Discussing the pattern of racial violence since the King rioting, Morris Janowitz has observed: "New outbursts appeared to be more goal-directed—a diffuse goal at times, at other times a very specific one. It is almost appropriate to describe these outbursts as political violence or political terror, or even conspiratorial violence. It is not inaccurate to describe this shift as one from expressive outburst to a more instrumental use of violence. Those involved were persons who came to believe that white society cannot be changed except with violence." (Hugh Davis Graham and Ted Robert Gurr, *Violence in America: Historical and Comparative Perspectives,* Report to the National Commission on the Causes and Prevention of Violence [New York: Bantam Books, 1969], p. 434.)

America will live up to its stated ideals and are on the verge of being radicalized, we must be sure what revolution actually is, and not confuse it with other forms or methods of political change. This problem is discussed in Chapter Two.

TWO

The Revolutionary Setting

REVOLUTION is that process by which an old social order is overthrown and a completely new order is set up in its place. This means that when we use this term to describe potential racial warfare in America, we are talking about a phenomenon that is different from all previous forms of American political change.

Initially the term "revolution" appeared in Copernicus' *De revolutionibus orbium coelestium* to describe the cyclical movement of the stars in their predetermined paths in the sky. In politics the metaphor of a recurring process that moves from the present back to some earlier, idealized, "better" condition is used by writers ranging from Plato to Machiavelli and Thomas Paine. In other words, up to the French Revolution political philosophers conceived of the various forms of political change merely as the necessary actions taken by the political "outs"—regardless of means or techniques—to restore the body politic to a previous condition of "grace." * As Hannah Arendt has noted in her classic work, *On Revolution*, the first time the notion of irresistibility—without any connotation of a return to an old order—was used to characterize revolution in addition to the usual conditions of violence, novelty, and beginning usually

---

* For example, the term revolution was used to describe the process by which the Stuarts were removed and the English throne was restored to William and Mary in 1688. This act, dubbed "the Glorious Revolution," was not really a revolution, but rather a restoration of the legitimate royal authority to its previous position.

associated with the term was on the night of July 14, 1789, when the Duc de la Rochefoucauld Liancourt told Louis XVI of the fall of the Bastille, the liberation of a few prisoners,° and the defection of the royal troops. The king's response was "*C'est une révolte*," to which Liancourt replied, "*Non, c'est une révolution.*" According to Miss Arendt, "Here for the first time, perhaps, the emphasis has entirely shifted from the lawfulness of a rotating cyclical movement to its irresistibility. . . . What is stressed now is that it is beyond human power to arrest [this movement] and hence it is a law unto itself." †

Miss Arendt's explanation of this event underlines the dimensions of America's racial revolution: "The king when he declared that the storming of the Bastille was a revolt, asserted his power and the various means at his disposal to deal with conspiracy and defiance of authority; Liancourt replied that what had happened was irrevocable and beyond the power of a king." Liancourt was correct, but the revolutionary analogy can only be directly applied to our situation if the conditions in twentieth-century America are sufficiently similar to those of eighteenth-century France. Unfortunately, they are. As in revolutionary France, the poor and hungry of the United States—largely, but not exclusively, black—are on the march. No longer are the ill housed, ill fed, ill clothed, and undereducated satisfied to remain out of sight and out of mind.

Whether the affluent white majority and its institutions will suffer the same fate as France's *ancien régime* and Louis XVI is a problem for all Americans. Miss Arendt's idea of irresistibility can be seen in the French, Russian, and Chinese revolutions;

° Edmund A. Walsh, in *Total Power* (New York: Doubleday, 1948, p. 147) notes: "The insurrection of July 14, 1789, and the storming of the Bastille did not, in the opinion of many contemporary observers, originate from the broad masses of the people but from engineered incidents and under the direction of mysterious personalities who suddenly appeared in Paris to stimulate and inflame the masses. The fall of the Bastille has been elevated to a symbolism comparable to the publication of the Declaration of Independence on July 4. But the cold facts of the record will show that when the fortress was taken, exactly seven prisoners were liberated: four forgers, two insane persons, and one young man guilty of such monstrous crimes that his parents had succeeded in having him imprisoned in order to save him from the death penalty. The reign of terror and the guillotine did not appear until four years later."

† Hannah Arendt, *On Revolution* (New York: Viking, 1963), p. 41.

however, irresistibility is not the same as inevitability. Perhaps, just perhaps, American society can end the old order based on white racism and establish a new one based on noncoercive principles. But before we deal with that issue it is essential to outline the necessary preconditions for a race revolution characterized by protracted violence.

The first precondition is awareness, on a broad scale, of the disparity between the "haves" and the "have nots." As long as the awareness is—or can be—confined to one group or the other there is little likelihood that the disparity itself will set the revolutionary process in motion. However, when both groups are made aware of this disparity it cannot be rationalized away as part of the "natural order," and then it can become operational.

In the case of America's racial revolution the blacks are acutely aware of the disparity, but the rationalizations to prevent white society's awareness are legion. It was only after the massive ghetto violence in Newark and Detroit in 1967 that the established political authority took a hard look at the euphemistic problem of "race relations" as expressed in civil disorders. It is to the credit of those who served on the President's National Advisory Commission on Civil Disorders (Kerner Commission) that they identified the principal cause of the disorders to be white racism and concluded that unless immediate steps were taken America would be further polarized into two separate societies, one white and one black.[*] Yet in the report entitled *One Year Later*,[†] prepared by still another commission, the authors concluded that the political establishment had done practically nothing to remedy the problems identified in the earlier report.

The political reality of the lack of action following the publication of the Kerner report lies not in the fact that President Johnson chose to ignore its recommendations, but that white society, both consciously and unconsciously, chose to reject the

[*] *Report of the National Advisory Commission on Civil Disorder* (New York: Bantam Books, 1968).

[†] Urban America, Inc., and the Urban Coalition, *One Year Later: An Assessment of the Nation's Response to the Crisis Described by the National Advisory Commission on Civil Disorders* (New York: Praeger, 1969).

awareness revealed by the report's findings. It may take a while longer for this awareness to become sufficiently broad and deep to become operational, but sooner or later the pictures—in living color—of Negroes looting stores will force even the most obtuse white or apathetic black to get the message.

A second precondition is that of solidarity among the potential revolutionary groups. Solidarity in this sense does not mean unanimity in the groups' goals or tactics but rather that in spite of their differences of opinion they are all deeply committed to change regardless of the status of individual members. In fact, in the incipient stages of revolution, fragmentation between competing groups may be worthwhile, according to Georgia State Senator Julian Bond: "The movement is surely fragmented, but in many ways it's a beneficial fragmentation. It means that if you're an integrationist and you have a program then you feel to work on it, a separationist has his program to work on, and so on. All these things complement each other—and on very crucial and key issues there's a great deal of unanimity." *

Whereas Martin Luther King and occasionally Ralph David Abernathy attempted to achieve solidarity among *all* the poor, and with sympathetic middle-class whites, subsequent leaders have been careful to use blackness as a base upon which to establish solidarity among potential revolutionary groups. Many white liberals are upset that they have been excluded from SNCC and CORE, but if the black revolution is to be set in motion, there can be no white faces or voices in such organizations. Much as the term "citizen" was reserved for the poor who took to the streets in the French Revolution, so are the terms "brother" and "sister" used to indicate that no matter what an individual Negro's current status happens to be, he or she is still a member of the family.

A third precondition of revolution is a system of myths designed to enhance the revolutionary group leadership's control over the masses and to provide the ethnological basis for violence. For example, the obvious immorality of slavery is exploited by the black revolutionaries to induce feelings of guilt, penitence, and contriteness on the part of the white majority

* Quoted in *Newsweek*, June 30, 1969.

and to produce solidarity among the black masses, even though slavery has no immediate bearing on the solution to racial problems.

Early in the revolutionary process the system of myths is particularly useful to the leadership of the potential revolutionary groups because the myths provide the basis for an emotional commitment to violence as the only means to achieve the groups' goals. Efforts by the existing power structure to dispel the content of the myths only reinforces the revolutionaries' claim of historical "truth" and distracts the masses' attention from any actions taken to redress actual grievances. As a case in point, both federally and privately finances projects designed to improve the condition of the Negro in American society are contemptuously waved aside by black revolutionary leaders on the grounds that they are only token efforts, and some insist that only the payment of reparations or "blackmail" for their ancestors' previous condition of servitude can spare white society, albeit temporarily.

A fourth precondition is the use by the dominant power structure of incommensurate and often unjustified violence against one of the potential revolutionary groups, rather than against a specific individual. Such action is readily incorporated into the system of myths, and in the course of continual retelling by the revolutionaries reinforces the fear and hate felt by the black masses toward white society.

Unfortunately, in carrying out the mandate of "law and order" too many public officials are unable to discriminate between actual nihilism and dissent directed not against the system but toward making it work better. Our leaders have had no experience in coping with dissent or division of opinion. They think the safest thing to do is to suppress it, but in fact they know of no other way to deal with the problem. This is their tragedy. But whatever the cause for their failure to respond to genuine demands, the result is to hasten the creation of yet one more of the preconditions for racial revolution.

A fifth precondition is an attitude on the part of the black masses of stagnation and despair toward any efforts undertaken by the white power structure to alleviate poverty. Essentially, this attitude is manifested in an almost stoic fatalism by the black poor. Notwithstanding the efforts of literally thousands of social workers, both trained and untrained, to work with the black poor, their attitude not only remains but is currently being reinforced by an emerging feeling among whites as well as blacks that the United States is deep in malaise and that neither the government nor the people have the power to do anything about the condition of the black poor.

Part of the problem in preventing this revolutionary precondition from becoming an active factor in the revolutionary process is the fact that the revolutionary leadership exploits establishment failures and attempts to sabotage those social programs that have any promise of success. To assume that the revolutionary leadership wants to eliminate the stagnation and despair of the black poor is to fall prey to the belief that the ends of an armed robber and a businessman are the same because both seek a profit.

During the land-reform program in Communist China, extensive use was made of the psychology of stagnation and despair to expand the Communists' control over the peasant masses. The Communists propagandized the peasants to believe that the harshness of their material existence was due to the avarice of the peasant landlords. This was not difficult to do because the peasants were ready to believe anything—anything but the fact that their farming practices and large families were more responsible for their pitiable condition than the land rent they were required to pay. It was a simple step to fix the blame for all wrongs on the hated landlords and then to incite the masses to murder the landlords on the basis of a local "people's court" decision. The value of this technique to the revolutionary was that after the masses realized what they had done they wanted to shed their guilt and were easily convinced to transfer both responsibility and authority to the radical leadership for any future actions to achieve the revolutionary paradise. It may be unthinkable now to consider a "black people's court," but it is not unreasonable to predict that the white slumlords would meet the same fate as their counterparts in Communist China.

A sixth precondition is the creation of a revolutionary organizational structure. Revolution aims for political power by special means, and its *sine qua non* is an organization based on the united front. Through the use of the united front the greatest weakness of fledgling revolutionary movements—factionalism— is offset by appealing to the lowest common denominator among the potential revolutionary masses in order to drop the net of organization over the widest possible base.

At present it appears that efforts to establish a single black revolutionary organization have been ineffective; however, this is consistent with the revolutionary organizational process because in the initial phase deliberate efforts are made to give the impression of a war among competing groups. Any genuine revolutionary group actively seeks to camouflage its efforts both inside and outside of its own organization. Competition is also used as a device to penetrate other groups and to identify any of their members who are impatient and frustrated with their own organization's efforts and who are susceptible to radicalization. On the surface the disagreements among the Urban League, NAACP, CORE, SNCC, RAM, Black Panthers, Black Muslims, etc. seem to indicate considerable differences of opinion with respect to objectives, strategy, and methods. Yet for all their differences, they agree about the insidious effects of white racism, which is simply the whites' refusal to accept Negroes as human beings, as social and economic equals, and this underlying agreement provides a "revolutionary space" large enough for the genuine revolutionary group to build its own organization and prepare to arrogate all the separate splinter groups under its control at the appropriate time.*

It must be emphasized that the use of the term revolutionary leadership does not mean that there is a single structure or organization heading up a black revolution at the present time. There are many organizations with the potential and aspirations to become the leadership group, but until one group is able or

---

* The revolutionary structure or organization operates within a revolutionary space that is established by the gap between demands and performance of the status quo establishment. In this book revolutionary space will be used as a synonym for revolutionary potential except that it will indicate where the black revolutionary potential lies in U.S. society, i.e., in urban ghettos where demands are going unheeded and where there has been protest for new policies. The goal of the revolutionaries is to exploit and expand the gaps of revolutionary space by expanding their own organizational structure into the space until it undercuts the existing regime's ability to meet the needs of the black masses.

willing to run the risk of exposing its long-run intentions, the black revolutionary leadership will continue to be made up of many groups.

Building a revolutionary structure requires attending to the boring and somewhat pedestrian task of social organization.* To this end, because the revolutionary structure initially is quite small, the most effective tactic is to promote the proliferation of local community-action organizations. If the first law of politics is to be re-elected, the first law of revolution is to control the people by forging them into an organizational weapon, for only after the people have been organized can they be mobilized and motivated to engage in revolution.

The seventh precondition is the failure on the part of the white-controlled society to fulfill the rising expectations of the favored minority of the black population who by virtue of their education might be expected to achieve a reasonable degree of upward social mobility in American society. Each of the preconditions is essential to racial revolution, but this is the key ingredient and the one which white society has the highest likelihood of preventing from occurring—although the hour is late.

The preconditions are general to the phenomenon of revolution, yet they are also peculiar to the problem of race revolution in the United States. From our original definition it can be seen that revolution in essence is change; however, there is scant agreement as to how much and what kind of change constitutes revolution. In spite of their profound character, the legal changes in America's race relations have not been considered revolutionary, although if they had been fully implemented perhaps America's racial revolution might have been accomplished without violence. But, as we have repeatedly seen, there appears to be no way to legislate morality or even to insure compliance with or enforcement of unpopular laws.

* The difficulty of this task is attested to by Stokely Carmichael, who has said: "Many people who would aspire to the role of an organizer drop off simply because they do not have the energy, the stamina to knock on doors day after day. That is why one finds many such people sitting in coffee shops talking and theorizing instead of organizing." (Stokely Carmichael and Charles V. Hamilton, *Black Power: The Politics of Liberation in America* [New York: Vintage Books, 1967], p. 105.)

The vocabulary with which an understanding of revolution is expressed has not been closely identified with the problem of racial conflict in twentieth-century America because our previous racial conflicts have not been revolutionary. They were not a struggle between the black minority and the white majority for a monopoly, or legitimacy, in holding—not sharing—political power, which is the current message of "black power." There is an irreconcilable conflict of interest. We are, in fact, two societies, and the black society has no believable basis on which to continue to accept white paternalism or even white-black "shared" power as the means to provide an open, free society. But for the black minority to prevail in such a struggle the revolutionaries must establish their claim to political legitimacy by providing a fundamental change in the way who gets what, when, and how.*

Before the reader dismisses the idea of a black minority's victory in a revolutionary struggle with the white majority as totally impossible (this will be discussed in Chapter Six), it is worthwhile to ponder Hans Morgenthau's question: "If a couple hundred thousand pajama-clad peasants can absorb all the power of the United States in Vietnam, how powerful is it?" It can be argued that the frustration felt by white America over its inability to impose its will in Vietnam has its roots in the implications of victory in our declarations of war on poverty, hunger, crime, housing, air pollution, etc. As we have learned—to our sorrow—declarations are not solutions or victories. To overestimate one's capabilities in any war is to lead to an intoxication with power.

To understand the phenomenon of radicalization in the revolutionary process it is first necessary to know what role the bourgeois elements play in the revolutionary order. The revolutionary order may be likened to a triangle. Each of the three points is separate and distinct and, until they are linked together, incapable of revolution. They are: (1) the revolutionaries, (2) the masses, and (3) radicalized members of the middle class.

* Harold D. Lasswell, *Politics: Who Gets What, When and How* (Cleveland: World, 1958) p. 62.

Although the principal concern of this book is with the problems of the black college student in his efforts *not* to become a member of the revolutionary order's triangle, it is also essential to examine the other elements to see how all three can be brought together to produce revolution. To this end, let us first consider the revolutionaries.

The revolutionaries are the spokesmen. In preparing for revolution they attempt to lead by speaking or writing. Their importance or influence at this stage is minimal, for they are generals without privates or lieutenants. Sycophants, ne'er-do-wells, myopic liberals, and social outcasts often surround the revolutionaries, but these persons are not the stuff of revolution or of effective social protest.

Among the current group of potential black revolutionaries are many types, ranging from the utopian black separatists to black nationalists. Each of these groups, although recently formed, has an essential ingredient for revolution, namely a historical and organizational tradition. The black revolutionaries' claim of a link with earlier efforts of the Negro in America to establish a separate political identity is not entirely valid, however, because until recently that effort has been one of concern for the well-being of the Negro and not his senseless sacrifice in a race revolution.*

Black nationalism in America has never been very successful, partly because of Negroes' ambivalence about their existence in the United States. This fact is pertinent to the black revolutionaries' efforts to exploit the tradition of black nationalism. For example, the early disagreement between the American Colonization Society, founded in 1816 in response to the actions of Paul Cuffee, a Negro sailor who in 1815 sponsored the emigration of thirty-eight free Negroes to Africa, and the Negro Convention Movement, founded in Philadelphia in January 1817, as to how or if the Negro should attempt to live in the United States has its modern-day counterpart in the argument between the integrationists and the separatists. The leadership of the Negro Convention Movement was made up of a small but vocal minority of educated Negroes who were opposed to the American Colonization Society on the grounds "that it had been

* See E. U. Essien-Udon, *Black Nationalism* (New York: Dell, 1964).

organized to remove systematically from this country all the free colored people in the United States." ° This group, which operated for three decades before the Civil War, summed up the dilemma of separatism for the revolutionaries when it said: "The question is not whether our condition can be bettered by emigration but whether it can be made worse. If not, then, there is no part of the wide-spread universe where our social and political conditions are not better than here in our native country." †

Significantly, as the Negro's search for identity in America has gained greater unity in recent times the voices of moderation in the tradition of Booker T. Washington and Martin Luther King, Jr., have been drowned out. This is consistent with the phenomenon of revolution, for there can be no acceptance of alternatives after the preconditions have been established if the revolution is to proceed. Thus, the black revolutionaries arrogate unto themselves the right to speak exclusively for the black masses and shout down the white and black moderates with epithets of "tokenism" and "Uncle Tom."

But who are the black revolutionaries? Are they paid agents of the Soviet Union, Castro, or Communist China? Are they "bad niggers" who have gone wrong as the result of some personal trauma? Are they like Spartacus, from the black masses they seek to liberate? Are they educated or uneducated? Are they genuine visionaries? Are they charlatans out for a fast buck at the expense of the black poor? Are they paranoids with an overdeveloped persecution complex? Are they reformers who mouth violence merely for effect? Or, finally, are they members of the select revolutionary fraternity who believe that violence is the only way to accomplish major social change?

They are all these and more. No single description can explain the black revolutionary, nor is a composite picture of the "average" revolutionary of much use in understanding their mo-

° John W. Cromwell, "The Early Convention Movement," American Negro Academy, Occasional Papers No. 9 (Washington, D.C.: American Negro Academy, 1905), p. 8. For an account of leadership of the American Colonization Society, see P. J. Staudenraus, *The African Colonization Movement 1816–1965* (New York: Columbia University Press, 1961).

† Martin R. Delany, *The Niger Valley Exploration Party* (New York: Thomas Hamilton, 1861), p. 6.

tivation. Analyses of what leads a man to become a revolutionary must be left to the sociologist and psychologist, and while such explanations are interesting and worthwhile, they are not particularly helpful in preventing a revolution or in stopping one after it is underway because the revolutionary's metamorphosis produces a new personality with entirely different compulsions. There is no way of telling in advance who among the potential revolutionaries will pass his personal point of no return. However, once that point is passed there is no doubt about who is a revolutionary, and his rhetoric and posturing betrays his purpose, vision, and fixations. His fulfillment is based on Armageddon, not the Cross of Calvary.

An excellent example of the radicalization process can be seen in the case of Robert F. Williams. Williams was the president of the Monroe, North Carolina, branch of the NAACP, and by all accounts was a moderate until 1959. That year, after two white men charged with brutal assaults on two Negro women were acquitted by the Union County (North Carolina) Superior Court and, during the same session of the court, a mentally retarded Negro was sentenced to imprisonment as a result of an argument with a white woman, Williams questioned the legality of the court. "We cannot take these people who do us injustices to the court," he said, "and it becomes necessary to punish them ourselves. If it's necessary to stop lynching with lynching, then we must be willing to use that method." He became more and more outspoken in his militance during the next few years, and his radicalization was apparently completed in 1961, when he fled to Castro's Cuba after being falsely accused of kidnapping a white couple. Williams was subsequently named chairman in exile of the left-wing terrorist Revolutionary Action Movement (RAM) and published an influential newsletter, *The Crusader*, which was widely circulated in the United States and among the black troops in Vietnam. He has recently returned to the States.

About the only thing that can be said for sure is that black revolutionary leaders are the generals and the general staff sections of an army with a doctrine, a plan, and a zealous devotion to their mission, but without troops and subordinate leaders.

Therefore, the second part of the revolutionary triangle is made up of the masses who serve as the troops in the revolutionary army.

The history of war or of organized violence may be described in terms of lines on a map, conflicting political or economic interests, changing technology, and so forth, but it also may be described in terms of those who actually wage war and do the killing. Until Napoleon's use of the *corvée en masse*, or conscription, warfare had been the almost exclusive province of the professional mercenaries, slaves, or the serfs in feudal society. However, following Napoleon's use of general conscription, all armies became more and more "civilized" in times of war in response to the necessity to field larger and larger armies. This process has a natural corollary in revolution, for the revolutionaries must of necessity rely on the total mobilization of the disadvantaged masses to destroy the existing government.

However, because of the state's near monopoly of the technology and armaments of warfare, the masses armed with broomsticks and barrel staves, as they were in the storming of the Bastille, have largely been rendered anachronistic. Even so, the development of technological warfare has not made the masses superfluous to the revolutionary process, but has only made necessary a redefinition of their role in terms of revolutionary guerrilla activity and perhaps made them the revolutionaries' secret weapon in an urban guerrilla war. Furthermore, the tactics of guerrilla warfare are admirably suited to revolution for they tend to mobilize the masses much more effectively than can be done by even the most dedicated revolutionary organization.

This point requires additional clarification because radicalization of the masses and the bourgeoisie lies almost completely outside the revolutionary leadership's ability and scope. For example, the black revolutionaries are inhibited in their plans because the black poor lack solidarity and are not sufficiently radicalized at this stage to do the dirty work of revolution—the killing. To be sure, potential revolutionary leaders can occasionally activate the masses to engage in a localized riot, strike, or demonstration, but before these acts can be integrated into the revolutionary process the masses must be prepared and organized to act on cue. But since the masses are fickle and not initially amenable to the discipline required to sustain a revolution, the potential leadership prepares them by a systematic organizational effort which from the point of view of both the masses and the prevailing power structure appears to be little more than unrelated acts of agitation. The leadership's design at this point is not to produce a tightly knit organization—for to do so would invite legal reprisal—but to prepare the disparate groupings for the imposition of discipline. Because this is an extremely subtle process, the normal protections of the laws against conspiracy are inadequate.

But to achieve the state of mind necessary to kill, the masses have to hate more than they fear, and to further radicalize the masses it is to the revolutionaries' advantage to provoke the police into a massive and indiscriminate response as the result of a ghetto incident. It is not our purpose to discuss the problem of police-Negro community relations, but only to say that the overwhelming majority of America's black community believe in the phenomenon of "police brutality" whether they personally have been the victims of a stationhouse backroom interrogation or police "bust" or not. The important fact for revolution is that police overkill reinforces the Negro's belief in the fact of two societies—one white and one black—and radicalizes the masses in favor of revolution. At that point the revolutionary group can claim to be the black man's protector from the police and inferentially from all of the white establishment's "Mister Charlies." The black revolutionaries' subtle exploitation of Robin Hoodism in the guise of protecting the brothers and sisters has great significance for revolution because it enhances the revolutionaries' claim to legitimacy and lessens the masses' fear of the state's monopoly of police powers.

While there may be some doubt as to who among the black revolutionaries will emerge as the leader or leaders of a black revolution, there is no doubt as to who are to be the common soldiers in such a revolution: the black poor. There is no need to belabor the point; other writers as well as government findings such as those embodied in the McCone Report on the Watts riot have repeatedly warned of the social dynamite inherent in our urban ghettos. But these warnings have gone unheeded. There are many excuses for not addressing the problems of the black poor with the same degree of national urgency as we did in defeating fascist totalitarianism, but no reasons. The situation is uncomfortably similar to that of Vietnam during the regime of President Diem, who for many of the same excuses failed to make the political and social changes necessary to merit the Vietnamese people's support. Numerous American advisers repeatedly pleaded with Diem to do the things required to build and maintain a democratic society, but he didn't listen—and he was killed.

To carry out the sophisticated activities involved in urban guerrilla warfare the revolutionary leaders need to acquire subordinate leadership capable of planning and controlling numerous decentralized, independent—although carefully coordinated—operations. This leadership must come from the middle class, for no other group possesses the organizational skills required to carry out planned violence. Since the rise of the middle class, the practitioners of violence have been forced to rely on it more and more to officer and lead their armies. And this applies even more in revolution because, by definition, the revolutionary must rely more and more upon man than technology in his equation of violence.

Thus, without active participation by the educated middle-class Negro, the black revolutionaries are not only the prophets of an idea before its time, but also the leaders of a revolution foredoomed to fail. It will not be easy for the revolutionaries to secure the active participation of the educated middle-class Negro, but they are patient, shrewd, and ruthless in their efforts.

THREE

The Black Student's
Academic Environment

THIS CHAPTER focuses on the academic environment in which the black college student is expected to resolve his personal identity crisis, prepare for his life work, and acquire perspective on societal problems.* To say that America's universities and colleges are sorely tried in their efforts to enable students—both black and white—to do these things is to state the obvious, but there is an added dimension for black students because education is their last and best chance to prepare for peaceful survival in the outside world. At the outset the college-bound black student must choose between two undesirable alternatives—whether to attend a basically inferior, predominantly Negro college or a

---

* The identity crisis which is at once both cause and effect of much of the current racial conflict is manifested in the terms black, Afro-American, Negro, and colored. The choice of any one involves not only a set of perceptions held by the observer to describe members of a specific race, but also reflects the observer's willingness to see those so described in terms of their own choosing. In this book, I am using the term preferred by the students themselves, i.e., "black." (How long black will remain popular as a word of racial identification has historical and social implications, because throughout American history racial as well as ethnic and religious identification have gone through cycles of popularity and disrepute.) The term "Negro" is used to connote "middle age," the status quo, complacency, and an acceptance of evolutionary improvement or inevitability.

school in which the emotional strain of being one of very few blacks in a white student body may outweigh or offset the value of a potentially better education.

There are approximately 107 four-year accredited, degree-granting Negro colleges and universities in the United States, the overwhelming majority of them in the Deep South. They range from the small local teachers' colleges with several hundred students to Howard University in Washington, D.C., with more than 10,000 students, founded by an Act of Congress in 1867.° In 1968 there were approximately 150,000 students attending Negro colleges and 95,000 attending predominantly white schools out of a total of 4,760,000 students enrolled full time in all accredited institutions of higher learning in the United States, or approximately 5.1 per cent. That means that 61 per cent of all black students attending college full time are in Negro schools.

Although Negro colleges may not have evolved from a conscious desire on the part of their various founders to create a separate but unequal system, this is how it has turned out. If the failure of the Negro colleges can be ascribed to one principal cause it is simply that Negro educators are not able, in general, to overcome the handicaps imposed on them by institutional racism. This is not meant to demean the accomplishments of individual Negro educators, who in spite of unbelievable handicaps have been able to "overcome," but—over the years—for every one who has been able to beat the system there are literally hundreds who have been brutalized and intimidated by it. Brutalization and intimidation have their own internal dynamism, breeding fear and antagonism in those caught up in a web of circumstances beyond their power to alter and control. Unfortunately, the Negro educator's failure has been seen by white society as due more to the limitations of the black students than to an inherently unequal situation. At best this is an

° Howard University was chartered by Congress and opened in March 1867 under the sponsorship of the Freedmen's Bureau. In 1929 Howard began to receive federal contributions on a regular basis. Congress made the reason explicit: racial segregation denied Negroes across the country the kind of education available at Howard. Federal support now amounts to about 56 per cent of the money the university spends annually.

example of a self-fulfilling prophecy made subconsciously by the white patrons who founded a majority of the Negro colleges and universities in the bleak hope that the mere provision of buildings constituted an effective means for black youths to acquire a worthwhile education and become full participating members in American society.

Another by-product of the Negro educator working in an environment fundamentally unsuited to the purpose of education° has been the development of hostility toward the black students on the part of the Negro educator. This attitude is not based on an unfounded intellectual arrogance—although some Negro educators are guilty on that score—but more on the fear of physical, financial, and social reprisal if he should dare to provide a genuine intellectual awakening to the black student. The Negro educator's personal and educational philosophy is summed up by the cliché "to get along you must go along."

In general, whites on the faculties of Negro colleges and universities are also culpable in the systematic enfeeblement of black education. What struck me at Howard, and was confirmed time and time again in conversations with black students, was that the white teachers resented and feared their own students to a degree that bordered on paranoia. The white teacher was concerned with the prestige level of his own rank rather than with the necessity and rightness of changes in black education. Together with the timid Negro educator, the white teacher at Howard would place the cold hand of death on any innovative proposal made by the students while continuing to proclaim his belief in nondiscrimination, good education, and equality. The result of this Negro-white cabal of incompetency is evident at Howard and other Negro colleges in that the turnover of competent white faculty members is almost four times higher than in similarly sized white schools. Inability to pay higher salaries is the reason given by the administration, but the written statements of those white teachers who have left Howard in the past five years reveal that the real reason is that they were unwilling

° The purpose of education is for the teacher to lead or draw out the student so that he develops the ability to understand the meaning of phenomena himself rather than accepting the teacher's—or other sources'—perception of meaning as dogma.

to continue to struggle in an academic environment that perpetuates rather than eliminates racial inequalities.

The black students know what happens to a competent teacher—white or black—who becomes popular. He either becomes fed up with the establishment's temerity and back-biting or is fired because of his advocacy of change and innovation. Yet in spite of the weaknesses of the Negro colleges, the majority of black students continues to attend them almost as if they believed in their ability to overcome a stacked deck.

To understand why the Negro colleges are inferior and produce—in the main—mediocre graduates one must go beyond the social alienation between black students and their teachers, because this phenomenon is an effect and not a cause. A look at the performance and failure of Howard University in providing black students with a higher education of equal value to that offered by comparable white institutions is most revealing. For if Howard, which is sometimes referred to as the "black Harvard," is unable to provide an equal educational experience for black students there is scant likelihood that any of the other black colleges—which are much less affluent—can succeed. It is not that Howard has failed to produce some outstanding scholars and well-educated graduates, but rather that it is the "C plus" graduate who is the true measure of a university's ability to equip the great bulk of its students for life after graduation, and in this area, Howard, like all the other Negro colleges, has failed.

At Howard the problem begins with the student body. In addition to having a larger percentage of foreign students (also predominantly black) than any other university of comparable size in the United States (between 1,200 and 1,400 out of a total enrollment of approximately 10,000), Howard must also contend with a distorted distribution of student abilities as measured by the Standard Achievement Tests (SAT) among the native-born black students. As the accompanying diagrams show, the scores of the majority of all white high school students taking the SATs fall somewhere in the middle of the curve, while the scores of native-born black students attending Howard indicate that four out of every five fall below the average white high school graduate; however, one out of every five is equal to or above the average white high school graduate.

All White High School Graduates
STANDARD ACHIEVEMENT TEST SCORES

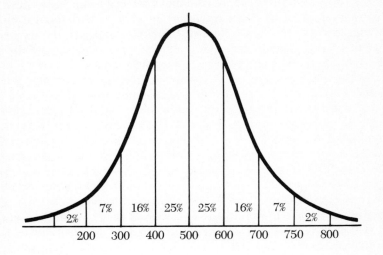

Native-Born Black High School Graduates Attending Howard
STANDARD ACHIEVEMENT TEST SCORES

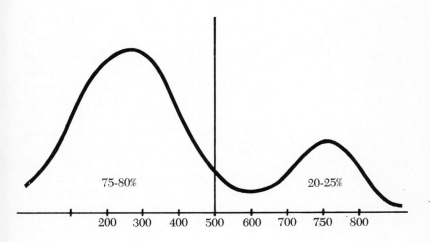

Even though the scores of the black students are not due to innate inferiority but to segregated inferior primary and secondary education,* this knowledge is of little help in solving the problem of how to provide a meaningful education for black students in a formally structured university.†

The student body can be best seen from the point of view of the teacher in a predominantly Negro college. If the teacher directs his teaching to the well-qualified 20 per cent, the remaining students become discouraged because they are unable to keep up with the material. On the other hand, if he is more concerned with the 80 per cent submarginal students, the better students become bored, "turn off," and fail to live up to their potential. Because there are so few of the so-called average students it is not possible to use a centrist approach. In a structured university the problem cannot be solved unless students are physically separated and taught on varying levels of intellectual difficulty until they are all able to participate on equal terms, but because of the higher costs and the social implications of multiple-track education, Negro college administrators and teachers ignore the problem and hand black college graduates diplomas of less and less value.

What struck me as I attempted to counsel incoming black students at Howard about their academic program in the fall of

* "Education in the slums and ghettos is a failure. Negro students fall farther behind whites with each year of school completed. Negro students start school with slightly lower scores on standard achievement tests by sixth grade they are 1.6 grades behind, and by 12th grade 3.3 grades behind. By 12th grade many have left: in the metropolitan areas of the North and West, a Negro student is more than three times as likely as a white to drop out of school by the time he is 17." (*One Year Later, op. cit.,* p. 29.)

† Those who seek reassurance that the Negroes' relatively poor educational achievement is based on genetic differences will find it in Arthur R. Jensen's "How Much Can We Boost IQ and Scholastic Achievement?" in the Spring 1969 *Harvard Educational Review.* Jensen's thesis that the IQ differences are almost entirely due to genetic differences between blacks and whites challenges the view that environmental differences and the cultural bias of IQ tests are the explanation for Negroes' poorer showing. The battle rages in scientific circles as well as in the political arena as to which view is correct, but for our purposes Dr. Jensen fails to explain why significant regression in black educational achievement in comparison with white performance has occurred in one generation. He offers no outside proof or explanation of a deterioration in black genes in the last twenty years, and yet he uses the IQ test data for that period to infer that there *has* been a genetic regression. To that contention, this author says, "Nonsense."

1968 was their ability to survive the personal trauma of being told the enormity of their academic challenge. For example, take the case of an eighteen-year-old graduate of one of George Wallace's "consolidated" high schools—"consolidated" in the sense that it put all the black children under one roof, in a building that looked good on the outside but whose intellectual offering was about on the level of TV's *Romper Room*. This student was the valedictorian of his graduating class, and his parents had worked hard all their lives to send him to college in the hope that he would be able to get off the treadmill on which they had labored. He was sensitive, honest, straightforward, and eager to acquire an education. He was not marginal in any sense among his black peers, nor was he inclined to view college as a battleground. However, when he was tested on the equivalent of the SAT he scored in the bottom 10 percentile of all high school graduates. Consider the emotional shock, after being the academic leader in your high school for four years, to be told, in effect, "You can't read, write, or cipher." This is the moment of truth for those who have been deceived by the charade of segregated inferior education.

The administration and faculty of Howard University and other Negro colleges are aware that the majority of their students are inadequately prepared for college work, but they are generally unwilling to acknowledge this fact openly because to do so would mean admitting the failure of Negro education. Instead, they ape the mass-production techniques of white schools and refuse to approach the individual student in terms of his unique gifts and perceptions. The tendency at Howard to do nothing—or at best to treat the problem in a superficial way by allowing the student to continue his education in spite of an unsatisfactory academic performance—is totally unsupportable. For example, approximately 30 per cent of Howard's freshmen students are on academic probation after the first semester, i.e., they do not have a 2.0 or "C" average; between 67 and 70 per cent of *all* students fail at least one course each semester; and approximately 30 to 35 per cent of the entire student body is on academic probation at any given time. Also, if the black foreign students, who make up 12 to 14 per cent of Howard's student body, and the members of other races are excluded from these calculations, we find that one out of every two native-born American black students is unable to meet even the lower academic requirements of Howard University's curriculum. One might contend that this reflects Howard's compassion in giving their students a second, third, and fourth chance to catch up but, on the contrary, it is damaging to the individual student because it creates an unrealistic expectation of achievement.

The students are aware of this problem and its damaging effect on their learning process, and the issue of the pass-fail system of grading in lieu of the conventional letter grades for nonmajor field courses was one of their "unreasonable demands" during the 1968 strike/boycott. Only after considerable rhetoric about "lowering standards" did Howard's administration and faculty agree to allow the students to elect the pass-fail option for courses outside their major field, but they made no changes in the manner in which courses were to be taught and set no standards to determine how pass-fail grades were to be assigned. The students were trying to find a meaningful way to assess their actual comprehension of their courses, and the pass-fail system might have been the answer, but the faculty and administration refused to do the hard thinking and work to implement it or to enlist the students fully in the learning process.

The only concession the administration made to the need for more individualized teaching was in the senior or graduate seminar, when it is usually too late to help the black students eliminate the formal intelligence gap between them and their white counterparts. The reason the administration made any concession at all was that they assumed that the students were so close to graduation that the full impact of ideas would not add fuel to the student-protest movement and that it was the appropriate time to "reward" them with almost full membership in a so-called community of scholars. Of course, one could argue, as I did, that the obverse of these assumptions was actually the case; but I was repeatedly told that our function as teachers was to maintain control and not let the students "gain the upper hand."

The education of the truly brilliant black student is largely self-determined or self-directed, and more often than not it is characterized by substantial gaps in fundamental knowledge. The point is illustrated by Howard's treatment of its so-called honors program.

The university has had an honors program for the past ten years, but it has been a program in name only because it has never been funded or organized to provide for the systematic development of the exceptionally well-qualified student. In the spring of 1969 the students enrolled in the program rebelled at the hypocrisy of running it on the basis of a once-a-week session where one of the fifty would present a book report to the entire group. They demanded that the honors program be changed to allow them to work under professors of their own choosing and to pursue directed tutorial readings in their areas of interest. The rebellion was successful only to the extent that the mass meetings were discontinued, but the program was not really changed to meet the students' demands because the university authorities made no effort to find the necessary money or make available the faculty to operate a really worthwhile program.

In May 1969 the honors-program issue was lost in the broader demands of the student activists for fundamental reform and the violence that shut Howard down for almost a week, but it remains a critical issue if the well-prepared black student is ever to acquire a quality education in a Negro college. It is just as damaging to a student's intellectual development to work below his capacity as it is to force him to work beyond his capacity if he is poorly prepared to handle college-level work.

The violence and physical destruction that erupted on Howard's campus on the night of May 7–8, 1969, was seen as no different from that on many other campuses across the nation, but this was not the case. The students acted out of an overwhelming sense of frustration with a university administration which had deceived them, obstructed change, and refused to act on the constructive suggestions they had made fourteen months earlier. One does not have to condone violence to participate in it if the provocation is sufficiently severe, as many basically nonviolent students did. Looking back on the violence some months later, it was all too clear that Howard's administration lacked both the means and the will to provide a meaningful education for the black student. The "will" part of the tragedy is under-standable even if it isn't acceptable, but the lack of means is a physical problem to which there can be a solution.

Howard, like many other Negro colleges, exists in a client-state relationship with white society in that it receives approxi-mately four-sevenths of its operating budget from the federal government in the form of a congressional appropriation. Other Negro colleges receive funds in varying amounts to meet their operating expenses from white sources such as the United Negro College Fund, private foundations, individual endowments, or state legislatures. The inability of Negro colleges and universi-ties to be self-supporting means that their administrators must approach "Mister Charlie" with cap in hand and head bowed to get the money to operate their schools. At best this method pro-vides education on the cheap, which does nothing to eliminate the discrepancy between Negro and white schools.

As a final note about the honors program, the dean of the College of Liberal Arts refused the students suggestion to seek money from private foundations or other government agencies to support an experimental program of direct tutorial training for exceptionally well-qualified students on the grounds that the potential benefactors would say no. It doesn't cost anything to ask, but the dean was either afraid or unwilling to risk a refusal. Such temerity is inexcusable, and it was manifested so many times and in such a variety of contexts that by the end of the 1968–69 academic year not only the underprepared but the well-prepared students had become completely turned off by the university administration's pointless posturing. It also provides fertile ground for revolutionary activists to take over and should be a warning to those who say they want to avoid a race revolu-tion.

At the end of May 1969, students I had come to know quite well during the preceding school year were afraid that Howard had passed the point of no return in its dealings with the stu-dent body. They foresaw more and more violence, less and less quality education, and no way for them to pursue their goal of a meaningful, useful, and relevant education. Theirs was a mood of resignation, more of sorrow than of anger, but they felt it wouldn't take much to turn them to anger.

Such alienation has an effect on the national scene because the black students are wasted before they can be effectively used by a society that needs all the talent it can find to solve its domestic and international problems. As Peter Drucker has noted, "However badly we need immediate mass production and craft jobs for the Negro, we need even more a massive effort to find, identify, develop and place the largest possible number of Negro knowledge workers as early as possible." Drucker also states that "the most hopeful development in America today is the rapid growth of the Negro knowledge worker in the last decades. Though still a comparatively small segment of the total Negro population—maybe a fifth or so—Negro knowledge workers have been increasing at twice the rate of white knowledge workers. *And for the first time the Negro knowledge worker identifies himself with the Negro community rather than attempting to escape it.*" * (Italics added.)

Drucker has provided the key to understanding the present-day black college student: if any realistic progress is to be made in solving our racial problem the real lead must come from members of the black community and not from the white liberal carpetbaggers. If the black student is to take this lead black education must be designed to exploit "native wit" as well as developing knowledge skills. Unfortunately, this split in the two aspects of black education has been emphasized by two competing approaches—Negro colleges set up as poor imitations of white schools as opposed to the so-called free-form storefront academies. The content or substance of the structured university and the free-form academies can and must be blended to meet our national requirements for persons who not only know the what and how of the American economic-political-social system, but also the why.

Because the black college student brings to his education an initial skepticism concerning the ability of white society to accomplish meaningful change, he is more finely attuned to the "why" in social processes than is his white counterpart, who by and large accepts white society's system of values, rewards, and methods. The difference between fact and promise is a major

* Peter F. Drucker, *The Age of Discontinuity* (New York: Harper & Row, 1969), p. 310.

factor in the American Negro's way of life, and this produces a revolutionary space in which the black college student can find refuge if he becomes convinced that the what and how of social processes are immutable. The revolutionaries seize the difference between fact and promise as a basis for their explanation that only the malevolence of white society is the "why" in all failures to effect change. If the black college student is to reject this narrow appeal he must have extensive knowledge about the capabilities and limitations of the American institutional structure as well as why that structure resists change.

Another reason that he should be made aware of these capabilities and limitations is that, with his firsthand knowledge of the what and how of the physical and emotional environment of the Negro in this country, he would be in a position to deal more effectively with the elimination of the underlying reasons —the why—for the continuation of the ghetto than George Romney and the Department of Housing and Urban Development. The hazard of a mediocre education for the black college student is that it leaves him less able to deal with the revolutionaries' propaganda and thus more likely to be drawn into a once-and-for-all violent solution to the complex problems involved rather than to choose from among the available nonviolent alternatives. In sum, a mediocre education for the black college student raises the significant probability of creating revolutionaries by default, rendering our racial problems less soluble, weakening our economic potential, and producing mental and emotional cripples in the black community.

Obviously the foregoing remarks apply more directly to the 80 per cent less-well-prepared black college students rather than to the 20 per cent who are better prepared to undertake a formally structured, white-middle-class-oriented higher education. The underprepared students have less opportunity to attend white colleges, although the "black ivory hunters" from the liberal private institutions, much like their slave-trading forefathers, are frantically trying to lure some of them away from traditionally Negro schools. Let us examine the well-prepared students who choose to attend Negro colleges.

The 20 per cent figure may seem too high or too low, but my own statistical analysis comparing the performance, on identical academic matter, of four randomly selected groups of about fifty students each—two groups of Howard students and two of U.S. Naval Academy midshipmen—revealed that 80 per cent of the Howard students scored substantially below the lowest midshipmen while the remaining 20 per cent scored well above the midshipmen's median. In fact, slightly more than half of the 20 per cent were clustered in the top 10 percentile of midshipmen scores, and about 5 per cent of the total black sample exceeded the highest scores made by any midshipman. In layman's terms these statistics translate into letter grades as shown by the following breakdown:

Grade	Howard Students	Navy Midshipmen
A+	5%	0%
A	6	10
B	7	20
C	2	40
D	0	20
F	80	10

Although these results reflect the performance of black and white students in an introductory course, Principles of Economics (a required course in both institutions), it is believed they correlate closely with other academic subjects as well as the subsequent performance of blacks in the economy at large, although academic performance, of course, is not the only relevant factor in explaining the latter phenomenon). For example, the data on distribution provided by the Equal Employment Opportunity Commission of the nonwhite work force shows that nonwhites are clustered at the lower end of the scale of skills and rewards.

Nonetheless, regardless of the fact that there may be some correlation between educational level and subsequent employment in white society, according to the U.S. Equal Employment Opportunity Commission the lower educational level of blacks "accounts for only about one-third of the difference in occupa-

Percentage of Male Workers
in Each Type of Occupation

Occupation	White 1966	White 1968	Nonwhite 1966	Nonwhite 1968
Professional, Technical, and Managerial	27%	28.8%	9%	10.2%
Clerical and Sales	14	13.2	9	8.8
Craftsmen and Foremen	20	20.9	12	13.4
Operatives	20	19.3	27	28.2
Service Workers	6	6.1	16	14.5
Nonfarm Laborers	6	5.9	20	18.1
Farmers and Farm Workers	7	5.9	8	6.7

tion ranking between Negro men and majority-group (white) men." *

Why does the well-prepared black college student tend to choose the inferior Negro college when he has the capacity to compete with some advantage in a white school? Both occupational and income statistics for blacks who are on an education level with whites indicate that they are subject to substantial underemployment, i.e., "the status of men and women who perform work which does not fully utilize their education, skills, and talents," but the statistics do not tell us *why* the well-prepared black college student chooses to become undereducated in a Negro college.

The answer is complex, but perhaps it can be reduced to the proposition that the well-prepared black students do not want a white education because they don't consider white society to be especially worth integrating into. The obvious corollary to this proposition is that the black college student would rather retain his identity as a member of the black community than embrace white society's standards, which would tend to make him *persona non grata* in the black community. Such a reaction is normal in our polarized society, for, according to Grier and Cobbs in their book *Black Rage,* "A brilliant high school student was awarded a scholarship to a prestigious eastern school. Despite the enthusiastic encouragement of friends and family, he chose rather a small Negro college of modest reputa-

* *One Year Later, op. cit.,* p. 12.

tion located in the South. He finally explained: 'If I go east, I can never come back.'" *

In such a case there is another problem beyond the loss of empathy with one's hometown black community. It is that a well-educated black man who returns to a southern community is subjected to even more discrimination than the underedu-cated person because he is an effective symbol of what the black man can do or can become; this strikes fear in the hearts of those whites who are committed to maintaining total control over the black man's environment. One exceptionally brilliant student put it this way: "I can attend Howard's law school, go back home and perhaps do my people some good, but if I go to Harvard [he had been offered a scholarship] they wouldn't let me take the Mississippi bar exam, let alone pass me even if by some miracle I did get to take the exam and scored 100." Per-haps such a view of southern intransigence is too jaundiced, but pressures such as these are very real to many well-prepared black college students.

Another reason that students choose a Negro college is that they are able to avoid many of the day-to-day emotional crises associated with the problems of race by remaining aloof from most of the black activists' agitation. It may seem paradoxical that a Negro college provides a relatively neutral refuge for the black student, but because confrontation between groups of blacks on a Negro campus is not in the activists' interest the in-dividual is able to defer his full commitment to the movement. This is not the case in a predominantly white school, where the black students are drawn together in response to a variety of so-cial and physical pressures.

A further consideration is the matter of cost. In the main, it is possible for a black student to attend a Negro college for ap-proximately a third to a half the cost of attending a comparable white school. The financial cost weighs heavily on the over-whelming majority of black college students, although not nearly so severely as the emotional cost of being the "duty nig-ger" at "Lily White U."

* William H. Grier and Price M. Cobbs, *Black Rage* (New York: Basic Books, 1968), p. 118.

Insofar as the idea of a separate, quality education for black students is a desirable goal, let us consider the proposition in terms of the so-called black university. There are those who will argue that any actions which smack of segregation are bad per se. Such an argument confuses means with ends, for if black capitalism—or, as it is currently called, minority-employment opportunity—has any validity in helping the American Negro participate and compete in the economic sector, then black education has an equally valid claim for national support. To be inhibited by form is to miss the point, which is that no substantive progress in bridging the gap between the educational level of whites and blacks can possibly occur if desegregation in education is pursued as a holy crusade regardless of the disastrous consequences arising out of forced desegregation.

The hard fact is that in the past fifteen years the American Negro is worse off in terms of his real educational attainment by every standard of objective measurement. To cite figures such as the percentage increase of blacks completing college or high school as a mark of progress without indicating both the absolute and relative decline in the quality of their education may assuage the white liberal's conscience, but it does nothing to help black graduates achieve genuine parity with whites. Perhaps, just perhaps, the black university can remedy this situation and in turn provide the well-educated black graduates that are so desperately needed in the secondary and primary school systems serving the black community.

An approach which recognizes the necessity to pursue quality black education as the means to achieve academic parity between blacks and whites does not mean there should be no attempts to eliminate segregation in other areas of national life. The point, however, is that even if racism were eliminated in other areas, such as employment opportunities, the American black would not be able to take advantage of those opportunities if he was—or remained—academically unqualified. The liberal assumption has been that institutional racism would recede like the tide in the face of a broad national effort, but what has occurred as a result of efforts to promote integration in education is that the disparity between whites and blacks has expanded, not lessened. It is too early to say whether competent black educators and scholars would support the education of their black brothers and sisters if the appropriate means were available. The Negro intellectual who has achieved sufficient "whiteness" is not particularly trusted by the black community, and those who have become token Negroes in white schools presently show little inclination to lend their talents to improve the lot of American blacks. But if the Negro intellectual's reluctance to become involved directly with black education is based on the lack of effective means rather than an "I've got mine" middle-class attitude, then quality black education has a chance for success.

What do we mean by a black university? Simply, an institution designed and operated to serve the real and total needs of the black community. The idea may appear revolutionary, separatist, or racist, but it is not since the black university would be concerned with all the forces that characterize, influence, and control the black community. Hoyt W. Fuller, writing in the March 1968 issue of *Negro Digest,* suggested such an institution should also be "concerned with the art of black people, and with the development and articulation of a black esthetic. It is concerned with the conscious strengthening of those institutions which make the black community viable, and it is dedicated to the liberation of black students (and black people generally) from the inhibiting and crippling presumptions which have been imposed upon black life and culture from outside the black community."

The value of such an approach is based, in part, on the fact that higher education in the United States is a bastard born of the attempt to couple the European idea of educating the elite with the American notion of educating the masses. Implicit in this concept is the deluded belief that a homogeneous population has been able to exploit higher education to considerable personal advantage. America's so-called melting pot process may serve to explain the educational emancipation of other ethnic minorities, but to assume that the American Negro has been "melted" and is profiting by the educational process is to ignore reality. Therefore, it is not unreasonable to accept the proposition that something is substantially wrong with the conventional approach to education insofar as it affects black persons.

There is considerable disagreement among blacks as to the

substance of a black university because of the varying approaches as to how best to serve the real and total needs of the black community. The arguments about the goals of a black university frequently obscure the issues because different groups define the needs of the black community in terms of their particular orientation. For example, the universalist ideal of a pan-black world comes into immediate conflict with the proposal of a separate black American nation-state. These issues are important, because whether the black university is to serve the needs of the so-called "Third World" or the needs of black Americans in a separate nation-state would affect the thrust of the educational effort. However, if the purpose of the black university is to serve the real and total needs of the black community as an integral element of the United States, the problem assumes manageable proportions.

Actions taken simultaneously on a broad front to identify, analyze, and assimilate the specifics of black social, economic, psychological, and cultural imperatives can be of considerable value in achieving educational parity between blacks and whites. This does not mean that basic education in mathematics, science, the social sciences, and the humanities would be neglected but that equal emphasis would be placed on the necessity for the black man to recognize and understand that he has a cultural heritage and identity in addition to the one created for him by white society.

Each ethnic group has added something to the world's cultural heritage. The black university represents the best available means for the black American to find out what part his forefathers played in that process. This is not a purposeless exercise, but is designed to fill the void of personal pride felt by blacks today who are neither wholly African nor full-fledged Americans because of the continuing influence of institutional racism.

The relevance of black studies—the systematic analysis of the whole complex of cultural, economic, social, and political values that characterize black people—is most frequently dismissed on the grounds that such an effort is not what the black American needs. For example, Bayard Rustin has asked, "What the hell are soul courses worth in the real world? In the real world, no one gives a damn if you've taken soul courses. They want to know if you can do mathematics and write a correct sentence." * However, Rustin and others miss the point because for technology or science to be relevant and not destructive of human life those who direct the applications of technology or science must be imbued with values in excess of those of the machine. There are many extremely able black scholars available to organize, direct, and control a valid educational effort in both the broad and specialized areas of black studies. Such an effort need not exclude white students or white participation in the form of financial support or parallel research, but for black studies to be effective white society has to keep its hands off the controls. Whites should become part of the effort if asked to participate by the black leadership, because black studies has more to fear from the arrogation and smothering of the effort by the prestigious white universities than it does from the revolutionaries' corruption of the concept for their own purposes. There is a simple reason for this: if white universities establish their own black studies program, the brain drain of black scholars from Negro colleges renders the black schools less and less capable of building a worthwhile program or carrying out other academic tasks associated with a college. There is something to be said for the fact that whites would profit from black studies, but because of the limited resources initially available to operate such an effort, the first priority must be in the black university so that the black student can study his own cultural heritage along with fundamental educational courses in a curriculum that takes account of his lack of formal preparation for college work.

Although a black studies program has as much intellectual challenge as Far Eastern or Russian studies, it has a broader intellectual purpose beyond mere academic exploration. To be able to understand oneself better in terms of one's cultural history is not a bad thing, but it is best done in company with those who can share the pride—or the shame. It takes some doing and perspective to live with the harsh realities of an idealized past, and for the American black it is best handled by black scholars. There is room for debunking in black studies, but whites would be ill-advised to throw even the tenth stone,

* AP report in the *Washington Post*, April 27, 1969.

let alone the first. To expect a full-blown curriculum in black studies at this time is ridiculous. To see just how ridiculous, all one has to do is to compare any current college catalogue of courses offered in any field with one issued twenty-five years ago. As knowledge accretes in any field there is an almost amoeba like splitting as man attempts to find out more and more about things hitherto perceived dimly or not at all.

Dr. Gerald McWorter, an Assistant Professor of Sociology at Fisk University, has suggested a structural outline that reflects the fundamental assumption for a black university, which includes a social (black studies) and an intellectual role. Dr. McWorter proposed three related colleges, each concerned with a distinct area but bound together in the concept of a black university: (1) College of Liberal Arts, (2) College of Afro-American Studies, and (3) College of Community Life, with separate centers of International Study and Conferences as well as a university press. As Dr. McWorter explained, "Each college would be organized around research, teaching, and practice. For every part of the university community there would be an advisory board of community representatives from all walks of life, with the task of providing policy suggestions and guidelines. This would insure the community of ties to the specific parts of the university."

Dr. McWorter's organizational structure for a black university is sound, but at present it is beyond the financial capacity of any Negro school to establish such an institution or to modify itself along these lines, nor is there sufficient state or private funding available to meet the higher educational needs of the black and the poor, and apparently federal-student aid funds have reached a premature plateau. To do what Dr. McWorter and others believe is necessary to make black education meaningful, the federal government must provide funds in sufficient amounts and on a regular basis to black universities.

Although a detailed cost analysis for a system of higher black education is outside the immediate scope of this book, certain gross figures will give some dimension to the problem. In the first place, if there is to be rough parity between the number of blacks and whites attending college the number of black students must be doubled, from approximately 245,000 to 500,000.

Leaving aside for the moment the distribution of black students between Negro and white schools, this would require an annual federal expenditure slightly in excess of $1 billion more than the funds currently being generated by other sources to pay for the education of black college students. If the current distribution between Negro colleges and predominantly white schools is maintained, the $1 billion cost figure would be slightly lower, perhaps as much as 15 per cent; however, because the physical plant capacity of the current Negro college system is not large enough to accommodate twice as many students, additional construction costs would have to be included. Obviously, many small Negro colleges would have to close in order to reduce the overhead costs of maintaining separate and economically inefficient institutions.

A black university system would encompass approximately twenty separate universities, each with a campus capacity for 17,000 to 25,000 students. It would provide approximately 70 per cent of the required black college student spaces, with the remaining 30 per cent provided by existing predominantly white schools. Schools such as Howard, Fisk, Tuskegee, and the newly founded Federal City College in Washington, D.C., could be the nucleus of a black university system, and new schools would be established on the basis of population distribution. The schools retained in the system would be expanded to accommodate additional students on an economical basis, i.e., with declining unit costs per added student, and ten to twelve entirely new campuses would have to be founded.

The dollar cost of setting up new black colleges from scratch is probably prohibitive in a political sense, but if the concept is acceptable to the public there are a number of existing federal installations that could be converted into college campuses at a relatively low cost—the superfluous military camps and forts which have outlived their usefulness but which are still functioning because of political pork-barrel considerations or to maintain separate military dukedoms for generals and admirals. For example—and there are many others—the Marine Corps recruit depot at Parris Island, South Carolina, is still open even though all of its essential functions could be carried out more effectively and at lower cost at Camp Lejeune,

North Carolina. To change Parris Island or any other military installation into part of a black university complex would probably cause apoplexy among the military establishment's hierarchy, but their temporary consternation is of little consequence if it is decided that meaningful black education is in our national interest.

Quite obviously there are constitutional as well as other political problems involved in "federalizing" a black university system, but none that cannot be solved if we are agreed that the proper education of black youths is of value to the nation. For if we agree that the answer to the question of who shall be educated is the one given by Dr. James Lewis Morrill, who pioneered the land-grant college movement, in *The Ongoing State University*—"not just . . . a well-to-do or intellectual elite but is . . . all who must carry the burdens of citizenship and productive service in a great and growing nation"—then we should not shy away from federalizing black education. The need is present and will not be met completely by either predominantly white state or private institutions of higher learning. To argue otherwise is to deny the performance of all the white-oriented schools in both the South and the North over the past thirty years. There are no exceptions to the statement that black Americans are grossly underrepresented in higher education. In 1969 there were more foreign students than American blacks enrolled in our nation's colleges and universities and, furthermore, according to John Egerton of the Southern Education Reporting Service, "The institutions which once were exclusively for Negroes still enroll a majority of the nation's black students and some of them, particularly in the states bordering on the South, are also far more desegregated now than almost any traditionally white college or university." °

There is another fact we need to consider about a black university system, and that is the role of the white teacher in a black school. There is no doubt that the existing supply of black educators with the required level of competence to teach in a

° John Egerton, "State Universities and Black Americans: An Inquiry into Desegregation and Equity for Negroes in 100 Public Universities" (Atlanta: Southern Education Foundation, May 1969), p. 93.

black university system is inadequate for even the current system, let alone one twice as large. This condition and the rate at which graduate schools are turning out black PhD's means that at least for the foreseeable future white educators will be needed to fill the faculty gaps in the black universities.* For example, the United Negro College Fund, which represents thirty-six private accredited institutions, has noted that in order to maintain accredidation at least 30 per cent of a school's faculty must hold doctorates. But the average of PhD's in the institutions belonging to the United Negro College Fund is only about 33 per cent, and if the white faculty representation were removed not one of the schools would be able to retain its accreditation.

This situation is further compounded by the phenomenon of the black brain drain, which is increasing at a rapid rate as white institutions—especially large state universities—are scrambling to recruit black PhD's at inflated salaries and academic ranks (with little or no regard for their experience) to relieve the pressure from both students and alumni to bring black teachers to white campuses. However, there is no valid reason for any white teacher to become a permanent member of the faculty of a black university until the *raison d'être* for a black university is accepted completely by white society. In the interim the more logical approach is the one suggested by the black educator Dr. Vincent Harding, Chairman of the History Department at Spelman College in Atlanta, who believes that joint appointments and visiting professorships could accomplish the same purpose and would be less detrimental to the black colleges. If Dr. Harding's suggestion were followed it would be possible to place competent white teachers in a black university

---

* A recent study indicates that although black Americans made up 1.72 per cent of the total enrollment in the graduate schools of arts and sciences in 1967–68, only .78 per cent of all the PhD's awarded by those institutions since 1964 have gone to Negroes. There is no long-term trend evident in the percentage of Negroes receiving PhD degrees, but the percentage has slipped from a 1966–67 high of .83 to less than .73 in the last two years. (Fred E. Crosland, Ford Foundation's Office of Special Projects, "Racial Enrollment Data from a Select Group of Public and Private Graduate Schools of Arts and Sciences," New York, 1969.)

without stirring undue fear in the hearts of the timid Negro educators concerning their job security and, perhaps even more importantly, to clear out the white faculty hacks from the Negro college system.

But the black university system is only part of the answer to the problem of providing black students with an intellectually challenging and socially relevant education. Steps must also be taken to make sure the students are as receptive as possible to this education, to counteract the inferior education they receive before they reach the college level. We must bring black higher education—and higher education in general—into the twentieth century. Regardless of the claims of college educators concerning the great changes in American higher education in recent years, there is still a vast technological gap between how students can be taught and how they are taught.

The application of currently available technology is the best single means to solve the problem of mass remedial training in the educational basics (reading, math, etc.) for the underprepared black student. Yet at best technology receives only lip service from both white and Negro educators. Their reluctance to use teaching machines or computer-programed consoles to lead students through a step-by-step learning process is understandable because no one advocates automation willingly for himself; however, until educators accept the fact that technology can perform many of the functions in the learning process better than they can, higher education will continue to flounder.

Experiments in the Boston area several years ago with teaching-reading machines by four- and five-year-old black ghetto children enrolled in the Head Start program showed that they could be raised to a third-grade reading level in less than a year. There is extensive research and work underway in the application of technology in the learning process, but this work is being conducted almost exclusively by private firms such as Xerox, Westinghouse, and IBM. Certainly it is proper for industry to work in the field of education, and the rejection and damning with faint praise of industry's efforts by the brahmins of higher education is at best short-sighted.

It is not only possible but economically feasible for private industry, in partnership with our system of education, to provide the means by which as much as 60 to 65 per cent of the learning requirements of a typical college education can be completed. That is, two out of three of the courses offered in a baccalaureate program can be automated at whatever level of student comprehension is considered necessary. Arguments about the depersonalised "brave new world" aspect of using machines in lieu of Mr. Chips miss the point completely, which is that Mr. Chips is spread so thin because of his outside interests and the necessity to deal with massive numbers of students that he has no time to deal with students intensively, either singly or in small groups. Teachers are a limited resource, and if they are going to be able to help their students realize their potential effectively it is mandatory that machines be substituted for teachers wherever possible. Furthermore, because a great deal of basic learning is repetitive in nature the machine is better qualified to teach it.

The black college student's deficiencies in reading, math, and even writing are more likely to be remedied by using technology in the ghetto high schools and Negro colleges than by any other method. No fundamental change in an institution's practices is easy, but if higher education for black students is not going to become the catalyst to turn those students into the lieutenants and captains of a black revolutionary army, the leaders of American education had better move quickly to adopt the teaching-learning techniques being developed by private industry.

We have discussed the environment of the black student on a black campus at some length—although not exhaustively, by any means—because the majority of black college students attend Negro schools. But what of the some 95,000 who choose to attend the supposedly superior white colleges and universities? Is the environment there less or more likely to produce black revolutionaries than that of the Negro campus?

Until recently the answer would probably have been "considerably less," because the percentage of blacks was minuscule on white campuses and the blacks themselves came almost exclusively from middle-class backgrounds and were generally superior students. But lately this situation, and thus the answer, has changed. A number of colleges and universities have inaugurated so-called "high-risk" admissions policies—that is, they are actively seeking academically underprepared black students from the urban ghetto and helping them financially with scholarships and educationally with special remedial programs.

This has created a problem on the campuses for all concerned. First of all, administrators generally make only minimal efforts to prepare the white student body to accept a relatively large influx of blacks (although still a small percentage of the total student population, a group of 100 to 400 low-income black students who tend to stick together can easily become a highly visible "critical mass" on any given campus). Since the student body reflects the racial attitudes of the population at large, a certain conservative, highly vocal element is likely to harass the black students. This in turn produces an understandably hostile response from the "high-risk" students, who are not inclined to feel grateful toward their white benefactors or to accept harassment passively, for to do so—in their eyes—would be to reject their blackness and play an "Uncle Tom" role.

The academically well-qualified students—the "superblacks"—become involved because they are automatically lumped together with their "high-risk" brothers whether or not they feel any kinship with them, merely on the basis of skin color. Thus they are continually confronted with very difficult decisions: whether to try to remain aloof from the other blacks, in spite of insistent pressure from both the blacks and indirectly from whites who consider all blacks the same; or to join them in an effort to assert their own blackness and as a means of protection, through solidarity, from the hostile whites; or to give up the white campus altogether for the academically less challenging but less emotionally hazardous black campus. There is evidence that they are choosing the latter course more and more often. It is easy to accuse these students of lacking faith or courage, but they *do* feel threatened and exposed, and they can count on little support or understanding from the university administration or the majority of the "middle-of-the-road" white students.

The problem of the "high-risk" blacks on campus is being exacerbated by a relatively recent phenomenon: following the

assassination of Martin Luther King, potential black revolutionaries significantly stepped up their recruitment efforts in urban
high schools. Thus many of the entering black freshmen, on both
white and Negro campuses, are "pre-radicalized," which certainly doesn't make them more disposed to accept without protest conditions and activities they consider racist in intent. The
high school recruiting-radicalization in May and June 1968, especially in Washington, D.C., was most effective in preparing
young blacks to assume an activist role in the 1968–69 school
year. Evidence of this could be seen at Howard University in
the fall of 1968, where there were 800 identifiable militant activists in an incoming freshman class of some 2,800 as compared
with only 200 in the entire student body in the spring of 1968.

The pattern of racial antagonisms resulting from an increase of black students on predominantly white campuses follows a fairly standard pattern which, although it becomes inter-
twined with the broader strands of the white student-protest
movement, still retains its own characteristics and produces additional problems as well as fruitful ground for potential black
revolutionaries to recruit students into their program.

First a black student organization is formed to promote solidarity (the national Black Student Union movement has been
quite successful). Then a demand is made for a black studies
program, which disconcerts the university administration, because for every white educator who is willing to face this problem there are ten who will attempt to evade it. This is to the activists' advantage, for it reveals the authorities' ambivalence.

During the battle for black studies, the black activists can
be counted upon to use the Students for a Democratic Society or
one of its radical offshoots, such as the Progressive Labor Party,
as its shock troops, but once the university administration capit-
ulates and agrees to include black studies in the curriculum the
black activists then set themselves apart from the SDS crowd.
This is a most effective tactic; it enables the black activists to
blur the distinction between black and white militancy on a
campus, enhances the black group's solidarity, and prepares the
groundwork for more symbolic black demands—segregated dor-
mitories and dining facilities and "soul" food. Predictably, arguments over the merits of such demands polarize members of the

faculty and administration, along with the trustees and white students. The tactic is old but still quite effective because a numerically inferior force must divide before it can conquer. And the more intense the polarization, the fewer chances there will be for any kind of communication among the various parties, much less any possibility of working together toward mutually beneficial resolutions to basic problems.

These divisive agitational tactics are relevant to the legitimate demands for educational reform being made by nonradicalized black—and white—students, because reforms have been delayed for so long that it is all too easy for the activists to exploit that delay for their own purposes. Continued delay increases the possibility that both "high-risk" and well-qualified black students on white and Negro campuses will be radicalized.

It is also very important that colleges and universities which have inaugurated "high-risk" admission policies include as part of their efforts a substantial, realistic effort to minimize the latent white student hostility (and white indifference) toward the incoming blacks and to do everything possible to see that they are accepted as full-fledged members of the campus community. Also, moderate and liberal white students could be brought into the recruiting process itself to start building mutual confidence from the beginning. And the administration, student counselors, and faculty should make an effort to be sensitive to any pressures the more right-wing students bring to bear on the black students once they are on campus. All these things, in addition to needed educational reforms, could help to neutralize the tensions inherent in integrated educational processes and the efforts of potentially revolutionary agitators. College officials are in no position to sit back and hope that eventually everything will take care of itself or that, with time, good will and reasonableness will prevail.

If we are to slow down or stop the process of black radicalization on college campuses we must act now, because the revolutionary space created by the inability of educators to change the academic environment to accommodate black students successfully is sure to widen in the months and years ahead. For as Yeats said:

Things fall apart; the center cannot hold;
Mere anarchy is loosed upon the world,
The blood-dimmed tide is loosed, and everywhere
The ceremony of innocence is drowned;
The best lack all conviction, while the worst
Are full of passionate intensity.

FOUR

The Black Student's Response
to White Society

THIS CHAPTER WILL FOCUS on the black college students' responses to and attitudes toward the institutions, organizations, groups, and power elites which make up white society as well as the students' perception of how those elements interact with each other and what role, if any, they see for themselves in that white world. In spite of the fact that their education may not have been the best, black students are not blind to the discrepancy between fact and promise in white society, and they understand the physical limitations of those institutions. Yet at the same time the students' lack of idealism, or, if you prefer, cynicism, colors their perception of the real—as opposed to the symbolic—capabilities of American society.

Before we begin our discussion, a note on methodology is required to place the responses and attitudes set forth below in some sort of perspective. Because what we seek to measure—namely, a man's boiling point—lacks the precision that would enable us to predict with certainty the conditions under which water will boil, the conventional, opinion-survey technique was rejected in favor of prolonged in-depth personal interview-discussions. With this method it is possible to analyze attitudes and thereby identify *relative* volatility produced by different types of social pressures. The lack of exactitude is not fatal to our purposes because if we want to reduce the social pressures which may cause the black college student to opt for the revolutionary solution, it is sufficient—and perhaps practicable—to deal with those pressures in a descending order of their level of irritation. Since social pressures are dynamic, what may be a major irritant to the black college student at one point may not seem so crucial at a later date. Thus I have not attempted to rate the pressures as to intensity, but only to identify as many of these irritations as possible. This is necessary if we are to make any attempt to prevent these views from turning into self-fulfilling prophecies after the students leave college. That is, if a black college student expects the best from an institution in his post-college life and this expectation is not fulfilled, black revolutionaries will exploit his subsequent disappointment and dissatisfaction, but if the student already expects the worst from an institution there is scant revolutionary space for the revolutionaries to exploit. Thus, the area of immediate concern for public policy can be defined roughly as limited on one side by the black student's cynicism toward America's institutional performance—past, present, and future—and on the other by his attitude of rising expectations.

In the course of interviews and discussions with some thirty students (of whom approximately two-thirds were undergraduate and one-third graduate students) a high degree of internal consistency was displayed by individual students in their attitudes toward institutions and race-related issues and activities if they had had some formal study in those areas. This tends to support the view that there may be a black college student "voice" and perhaps that the beliefs and perceptions of the students concerning race-related issues and activities can be altered if the real difficulties in solving our social problems are presented fairly and objectively to them. This tentative conclusion is both encouraging and alarming because it renders the black college students as a group susceptible to indoctrination or education by organizations that may either be violent or nonviolent in their orientation and basic purpose. This is not to say that the *individual* black student is ready, willing, or able to follow a revolutionary Pied Piper, but it does mean that a condition exists in which revolutionaries could make effective use of mass evangelistic recruiting techniques rather than being confined to personalized recruitment methods.

The following attitudes and responses are a composite of a series of interviews that have been blended together, where possible, to set forth generally held positions as well as what specific individuals think about their future relationship to the institutional structure of American society. It is possible that I may have misinterpreted these views, but I think not, for I have not attempted to speak for the black college student in the formal role of an advocate, but only to report as accurately as possible what sincere, honest, intelligent human beings have told me—as just another human being—about their understanding and evaluation of the world in which we both must live.

In the following discussion only those elements of America's institutional structure that are relevant to our revolutionary potential are considered.

Of all the elements which make up the American institutional structure, the one toward which the black college student holds more definite and more complete ideas than any other is government. Their understanding ranges from a perception of the abstractions underlying the principles of representative democracy to a rather full awareness of the deals and petty corruption which characterize government at the local and state levels for the black American.

The students' view of American representative democracy tends to reflect a view of man as power-seeking and violence-prone rather than reasonable and compassionate. This perception may be colored by the black experience in the United States, but it also reflects a deep appreciation of what *is* rather than what *ought* to be. For example, the great bulk of the students saw the GOP's seeming indifference to the black vote in the 1968 election campaign more as an exercise in comparative arithmetics than as one in comparative political philosophies. They believe that in American political philosophy the simple arithmetic of the blacks' minority position coupled with their lack of economic and political power provides the rationalization not only for white majority rule, but, more importantly, for white majority control. In their minds, the conflict between white majority rule and black minority rights will remain one-sided because for the white majority to surrender or share any of its power with the black minority would be logically inconsistent.

One student who argued unsuccessfully for SNCC to support George Wallace for the Presidency put it this way: "The black voting minority has no continuing power base and so no pay to them is required in terms of legislation, programs, and so forth. What the blacks receive, they receive out of a sense of *noblesse oblige* by those who come to or are in power, or as a concession to their potential for violence. The Republicans have added up the votes which can be expected from their sources of power and have concluded that this total is enough to elect Nixon, and they see no need to risk any dilution of that total by appealing to blacks—that is, there's no advantage in getting one black vote if it costs you two white ones. On the other hand, the Democrats, in recognition of the GOP strategy, conclude that the black voter has no place to go but with them and so why bother to pay off blacks with any added concessions?"

This student, who talked to me six weeks before Nixon's so-called southern strategy was fully revealed by the election results, felt that blacks could wield real national political power only by supporting Wallace. As he explained it: "If the black voters could be persuaded to vote as a bloc in the southern and border states for George Wallace then the major political parties would be forced to make more concessions to blacks because if the black vote didn't go as planned neither of them would be elected."

Another student put it more prosaically: "It used to be that the black man could get along as long as there was peace and quiet in the white man's world, but today the better way to get along is to have the white men fighting among themselves—then they won't have any energy left over to give the black man a hard time."

One might encounter, as I did, that internecine white conflict might slop over and include the black community or that the black man might become the scapegoat in a white political conflict, but the student was adamant in believing that the potential gains of white divisiveness far outweighed those of "consensus" politics that treats the black man as even less than a poor relative when it comes to cutting the political pie.

In many ways the students' views of American representative democracy are not at odds with either the theoretical propositions underlying that concept or the Fourth of July rhetoric that surrounds it. Their views, in fact, anticipate a significantly broadened political pluralism and reflect the remarkable diversity of America, which needs political representation that is not based on conventional expressions of power but on individual men. The students are still groping for a full definition of this idea, but they are not optimistic about the ability of the established national political processes to be effective in reaching the goal of a more personalized political pluralism. With one exception (and that one for reasons that had nothing to do with a more humanistic approach to government as government), all the students categorically rejected for themselves a career in the Senate or the House of Representatives because they felt that elected officials on the national level were unable to accomplish any meaningful or permanent change in the face of the power blocs which elected them as well as the relative impotency of Congress vis-à-vis the executive branch of the federal government. This is a significant finding because it reveals that the students think Congress is not only ineffective but that it is subordinate to the executive branch, a belief that may or may not conform to reality.

One student who dismissed congressional efforts in behalf of the black minority as inconsequential phrased it this way: "I've been working part time and full time for the past three years for my Congressman [who happened to be one of the Democratic Party's leaders in the House], and he's nothing. He's a personally agreeable, gentle, honest person but outside the House he has no real power to make anything happen. Occasionally he can, and does, give a second-string bureaucrat a hard time in a committee hearing about some minor agency foul-up, but that doesn't really count for a hill of beans because those agencies go on like Old Man River. Any one of us blacks from school who work on the Hill for a Congressman or Senator [there are about 150 students at Howard so employed, and the sample of thirty from which this discussion was derived included seven of them] knows that this isn't the Age of Aquarius but the Age of the Agency. That's where the money is—and that's where the power is."

How do the students see the role of the federal agency or department in relation to the President and to the black minority, and how hopeful are they that the agencies will be able to accomplish meaningful reform or promote broad-based political pluralism? Answers to these questions go to the heart of the black college students' rejection of the "old politics" as retrospective and sentimental and their espousal of the new politics of black political power, which they see as forward-looking and realistic.

To the black college student the President of the United States is primarily an object of condescension, and they are very skeptical of his ability to do anything to improve the condition of the American black. They make little distinction between presidents, whether Lyndon Johnson or Richard Nixon, although they feel a little more warmly toward John Kennedy, not so much for what he did for the blacks but because he was the brother of Robert Kennedy, who captured their imagination. They feel that the President is too restricted by either partisan requirements or bureaucratic red tape to carry out meaningful reforms. As one student said, "No, I don't believe the President is two-faced about what he says he wants for the black people; it's just that no matter what he wants he can't move the bureaucrats unless the bureaucrats want to move."

The belief that bureaucratic inertia is an effective brake on social reform at the national level is consistent with the students' opinion of elected officials and raises the question of whether the students think the government is at all capable of acting positively to promote social reform. The answer is that they see the government as a passive ingredient in the entire social process rather than as an innovator, and their skepticism extends to the appropriateness of government actions taken supposedly in behalf of black Americans. For example, one student said, "As long as I can remember my father has been a big man in the civil rights movement. He's made a big thing—and a good living—out of the movement by serving on committees, explaining to white liberals what the Negro wants, and in general being a 'spokesman' for the black community in spite of the fact that we've lived in a white suburb for the past fifteen years and have become more white than black. But what I can't understand is why he and all those blacks and whites who've been working in civil rights thought that the way to solve the problem was to pass more laws."

This view was widely shared by other black students and illumines the central theme of their response and attitudes toward government, which is a feeling of alienation because of government's failure to enforce the policies it proclaims as the law of the land rather than because of its ineptness in carrying out socially oriented programs. The spate of civil rights legislation is seen as a cruel and unnecessary deception for black citizens because the federal government raises false hopes and attempts to make it appear that the lack of civil rights for Negroes is due to a lack of laws rather than an unwillingness to apply existing laws, such as the Constitution. They see no value in symbolic legislation or in high-level statements of intention about racial matters when both the legal basis and the techniques to eliminate institutional racism have existed so long but have not been used by one President after another.

From a revolutionary standpoint the students' low expectations concerning the federal government's seeming unwillingness to use the law as a means to eliminate institutional racism has little significance in the radicalization of the black college student; however, if the black students should come to feel that the federal government is selectively using the law as a punitive weapon to eliminate black-power groups, whether they are members of these groups or not, their relatively neutral skepticism is more likely to become active hostility.

The black students have a good idea of the federal government's specific "geography and climate," at least to the extent of how hospitable the different agencies are to the presence and employment of black Americans. Given the attitudes of the black college students toward government it may seem incongruous that any of them would consider it as a potential employer on any level, state, local, or federal. Nevertheless, government is the immediate as well as the employer of last resort for more than three out of four of all black college graduates at least once in their overall work experience. Their choice of government employment, although largely confined to low-level management and routine clerical posts, is based partly on the fact that it is considered "safe" and not usually subjected to white reprisals, and partly on the fact that there is a rather substantial although unorganized black intelligence apparatus concerning the availability of government positions, working conditions, and the color pressures in the different agencies and departments. These conditions range from a description of "strictly soul" in the Department of Agriculture, which has the highest percentage of black employees next to the Post Office Department (historically a refuge for the American black), to the "lily white" Department of State, which in spite of extensive experience in dealing with persons of other races and nations hasn't been able to figure out a meaningful place in its domestic or overseas operations for black Americans.

According to the students, the acceleration of the trend to employ blacks in government is due more to an attempt to achieve more than a token appearance of integration and to the fact that more blacks were applying for—and *staying* in—Civil Service posts rather than a conscious effort to expand the participation of blacks in meaningful jobs at all levels. One student who had access to internal memoranda in the Civil Service Commission said that the government's leadership was most concerned over the fact that fewer and fewer whites were taking the Federal Service Entrance Examination (FSEE) while the number and percentage of blacks entering government was increasing, as were the number and percentage of blacks remaining in government service for more than a year.* The gross figures indicated that the percentage of blacks entering government service by way of the FSEE has increased by almost threefold in the past eight years and that during the most

---

* The Federal Service Entrance Examination is much like the standard educational achievement test and is used as an initial screening of prospective employees in the federal government for college and high school graduates who desire to become a part of the nation's bureaucracy in other than physical assignments such as truck drivers, printers, etc. Failure to pass the FSEE precludes appointment to a professional or "register" position or to the paper bureaucracy.

recent year more than one out of three new employees—those with less than one year of service—had resigned; however, only one out of twenty who resigned was black. This situation, the student reported, prompted one official to conclude that if the trend continued, the federal agencies would soon "become bodies with white or *café au lait* heads and black bodies."

The more militantly inclined students in our sample recognized the potential for disruption in the pervasive black presence in the federal government, but they had no ideas as to how that potential could be used in a positive way to help black people as long as whites continued to monopolize control over government programs. However, one student who had formerly been a member of one of the more revolutionary-oriented black organizations said that activists considered the ever-expanding numbers of blacks in government as their "volunteer" intelligence service to keep them informed about federal intentions in matters important to the black community and their organizations.

In sum, the black college students' composite attitude concerning federal government employment seems to be that it is an "easy" way out and a means of achieving some measure of financial security, and it will make fewer demands on them as blacks for performance; there was a tacit belief in the idea that "if you can't beat 'em, this is the cheapest and easiest way to join 'em." They reject, almost out of hand any real hope that government will do anything concrete in behalf of social processes, but, in terms of radicalization, their acceptance of government employment is more passive than active. The tragedy, however, is that the black college students see government more as an escape than an opportunity to fulfill themselves as creative, unique individuals.

At the state and local level the black college students' view of government is not nearly so benign. Although most people's understanding of institutions is usually somewhat vague and elusive, the black students' perceptions of state and local governments are clear and precise. Students see them as essentially racist institutions organized to enforce and perpetuate the white status quo, a view based largely on the use of "states rights"—in both the North and the South—to deny black Americans their civil rights and on the shameless economic exploitation of blacks that can only be carried out with the connivance and sanction of elected and appointed state and local officials. These views translate into a feeling of fear concerning the students' economic well-being as well as their personal safety in many cities and states, and this fear has significant revolutionary overtones, because it is but a step from fear to hate if there is no way to separate oneself from two or more contesting forces.

In the strictest sense, it is not possible to separate the students' view of the institution of state and local government from its functions, such as law and order, community services, and education. Where they see the federal government as made up of essentially nonrelevant agencies operating in a partial vacuum unable to translate dollars into meaningful action for black people, they see an immediate causal relation between state and local dollars and action or inaction. For example, the failure to provide equal educational facilities, police protection under due process, garbage collections, sewage, and road repairs in black communities is personalized—that is, Mayor X or Governor Y didn't do it, or *he* spent the tax money with little or no regard for the needs of black people. They do not feel this kind of personal antagonism toward the President or his cabinet officers.

Individually and collectively the students of the sample rejected the idea that state and local governments could accomplish meaningful change or reform in American society until the blacks were able to exercise political control over the expenditure of public funds. They could not conceive that the white political power at the state or local level would share their power with the black minority or act to insure equitable distribution of government services and functions. This cynical attitude was not modified by the elections of such men as Julian Bond to the Georgia state legislature, Richard Hatcher as Mayor of Gary, Indiana, Carl Stokes as Mayor of Cleveland, or Charles Evers as Mayor of Fayette, Mississippi, which were considered to be aberrations that would not, or could not, survive a white counterattack.

Thus, in conclusion concerning the black college students' attitudes toward government, a composite picture emerges that includes a curious mixture of toleration, condescension, neutrality, fear, and latent hostility. The students feel little or no personal identification with the institution of representative democracy, nor do they have much faith in its ability to effect change or improve the position of blacks in American society. Whether or not these views are too pessimistic, what is important in the revolutionary context is that the black college student does not believe he has a personal stake in the continuation of our democratic system, no matter how badly or how well it might function at some future time. And to tell these students, who have yet to participate fully in the democratic process, that alternative forms would be worse is not only paternalism at its worst, but foolish as well, because to do so provides the revolutionaries with the ammunition they need to woo recruits to their cause.

The large majority of the black college students think of the military in almost the same terms as professional military men use about the civilian world—that is, as the "outside." Their attitude is best described as dissociative: the goals, aspirations, and hopes of a professional soldier seem as alien to the black college student as those of a member of England's House of Lords. There is little or no antagonism toward the professional military as a group, even among those students who have served in the armed forces, but they are keenly aware of the strong southern bias in the ground forces of the Army and the Marine Corps as opposed to the more national orientation of the Air Force and the Navy. Aside from widespread complaints concerning the behavior of sergeants—with or without racial overtones—they see the military as a neutral to favorable element in the racial equation. This outlook, in turn, derives from an appreciation of the officer corps's professional necessity to avoid charges of racial discrimination and the increasing percentage of blacks in the regular armed forces, even though they are mainly in the enlisted ranks. Both of these facts have importance in keeping the military as an apolitical force in local racial situations, but because the expansion of the number and percentage of blacks in the armed forces has considerable significance in any future race revolution it will be discussed in detail in Chapter Six.

The dissociative feeling about the military is also based on a broader view that it is impossible to justify the international actions of the United States while domestic problems go unheeded. For example, with only one or two exceptions, the sample of students did not reject the Vietnam War on moral grounds, but because it diverted resources from the solution of problems confronting black Americans. One student, active in intercollegiate political activity, observed: "The white kids in the SDS just don't understand the blacks' idea, which was that although stopping the killing in Vietnam would be a good thing it couldn't possibly command the attention and efforts of black students until—and unless—the figurative and in some cases the literal killing of blacks in the United States was stopped first."

Also, in evaluating the military side of the so-called military-industrial complex, the black students did not see the military's role as part of a giant conspiracy to deny the blacks their due. As one student said: "They're doing their thing, and they believe in it—which can't be said for most of those who oppose war, regardless of what they say."

This latent neutrality toward the military as an abstract, almost apolitical force insofar as it affects black lives was fairly widely held by those in the sample. However, on the other hand, this live-and-let-live attitude did not extend to the National Guard, which was consistently seen as the "lily white" arm the state governments used to enforce the will of the white majority on the black minority.* There was no confidence that

---

* The students' view is reinforced by the fact that after overwhelmingly white units were used in the summer of 1967 to stop Negro urban riots, the Kerner Commission recommended to President Johnson that immediate steps be taken to raise Negro participation in the Army National Guard substantially above the token 1.24 per cent it was at the time, but nothing of substance has been done. Department of Defense figures released on March 23, 1969, show that the number of Negroes in the National Guard declined from 5,184 at the end of 1967 to 4,944 at the end of 1968 out of a total strength figure of 391,000. In the 1967–68 period Negro membership in the National Guard declined in twenty-five states, including a dozen in the North and Midwest. The statistical distortion is even more severe than the token average of 1.24 per cent reflects because in fifteen of the fifty states there are only .1 per cent or less Negroes in those states' units. No attempt is made in any state to maintain racial balance in the National Guard on the basis of population, and until the passage of the Civil Rights act of 1964 Negroes were formally barred by state law from joining the Guard in five southern states.

the National Guard would protect the black population in the event of either black or white activist violence. In most cases these views were not based on an abstract concept of the National Guard; because of their experience with civil rights organizations, more than half of the sample had been able to observe the Guard in action in both northern and southern states. In addition to being skeptical of those who direct and control the National Guard, the students were also clearly dissatisfied with the level of professional competence displayed by Guard troops in carrying out anti-riot and protective functions. One student who had served in the Regular Army for four years with eighteen months of combat experience in Vietnam contended that the use of the National Guard in any racial confrontation was more likely to prolong or expand the trouble than any action the authorities might take to quell the disorder.

Finally, the students of our sample did discriminate between the National Guard and the regular military establishment in that their antagonism to the Guard did not extend to the regular military. Furthermore, they were unanimous in the opinion that if civil disturbances did arise which required the use of troops to restore order such troops should come from the regular forces to insure that no reprisals would occur against members of the black community and to avoid that fatal "first shot."

Parenthetically, it should be noted that the students' attitudes toward the military, and especially about the National Guard, reflect an acceptance of legitimate power coupled with a keen awareness of the hazard of wielding that power without the effective constraint of responsible supervision in matters affecting black people. On a related issue of military legitimacy, they did not have an especially race-oriented attitude about the draft and military service. They did not agree with the black activists that the white man is drafting the black man to fight his wars, nor did they reject out of hand the idea that blacks could take advantage of military service as a means to acquire the training and experience needed to compete in American society. This very pragmatic view is also reflected in the fact that voluntary ROTC programs are still extremely popular in the Negro colleges and universities in spite of the widespread anti-ROTC activities in white schools; in fact, as of June 1969 nearly half of the sixty colleges which wanted to establish ROTC programs on their campuses were Negro schools.

This situation, together with the increasing number of officers being commissioned from the ROTC program from the Negro colleges and universities, is further evidence of the pragmatism of black college students when, without pressure or coercion from outside sources, they evaluate a situation or institution in terms of their own conception of what is in their best interest. One student noted that after the two-year compulsory feature of the ROTC program was eliminated at Howard University, more students enrolled in the four-year program leading to a commission in the Army or Air Force. Furthermore, he added, those who took part in the ROTC program were under little or no social pressure from the more militant student activists on the campus in regard to their "militarism." This toleration of ROTC and voluntary military service is significant because it may provide an additional means by which the skills of black students are upgraded through their participation in the professionally and academically oriented military-training programs as well as a leavening force to prevent the politicizing of the armed forces on racial issues and activities. This is not to say that the black college students' apolitical pragmatism in this area will remain favorable if the increasing polarity of white to black in and out of the military service should result in white officers and noncommissioned officers failing to comply fully and completely with President Truman's 1948 Executive Order, which stipulates equality of treatment and opportunity in the armed services for all races.

In sum, black college students have not prejudged the military system, nor have they rejected its worth insofar as it can assist them in meeting their life goals, but it—like any other institution of white America—is on trial in their eyes.

The next institution of white society that we investigated was the free-enterprise system. The students' attitudes and opinions about free enterprise differ substantially from those about government and the military because the black college student does not have the knowledge and experience to evaluate business operations in a socially relevant context, i.e., how business policies and actions affect the lives of black people in general and themselves as individuals. Part of this lack of understanding of what business is all about is directly attributable to the non-business orientation—and, in many cases, the anti-business orientation—of Negro colleges and universities. For example, although some of the large schools offer a few courses in business administration and related subjects, it is not possible for a black college student to pursue an integrated degree-granting program in business administration at any Negro college or university.

Even though black students have little direct experience with American business, their views on the subject can perhaps provide us with a possible solution to our racial problems. Time and space preclude a full analysis of black-activist propaganda in this context, but the greatest opportunity to make the radicals look ridiculous is to challenge their vocal and written denunciations of the "fascist capitalists."

The sample of students unanimously admired the ability of American business to produce the material ingredients of the "good life." They did not clearly understand the "how" in a technical—or even an ideological—sense, although they were more tolerant than their white counterparts of the legitimacy of making an honest profit. In discussion after discussion, the students refused to be dissuaded from their belief in the capacity of the free-enterprise system to make innovative social changes, in spite of its reputed lack of social responsibility, its "grasping capitalists," "establishment control," or any other cliché-ridden arguments, because, they said, "If the American businessman has to choose between his profits and his prejudice, he is going to choose profits." In fact, the students regarded business as the only major American institution that had the ability, if not the desire, to make positive changes for black Americans.

The black students' behavior with respect to corporate recruiting is most revealing. Several years ago, corporate recruiters found black students lukewarm toward entering the business world, but today, with the increased competition for college graduates, and particularly for black college graduates, the students are more interested in jobs with corporations. More than 150 American business, manufacturing, and financial concerns systematically recruit at least once, and in many cases twice, a year from the Negro colleges and universities; at no Negro college or university—even those at which there has been considerable student activism or disturbance—has any recruiter been prevented from talking freely with all students who wanted to discuss employment, nor has there been any protest directed against any recruiter or his firm. The fact that the Dow Chemical Company is able to recruit black students on a black campus without any trouble should be remembered when black and white student protesters are lumped together in one group by right-wing politicians. The same courtesy and open-mindedness has been shown by black students to recruiters from the CIA and the FBI.

After discussing the prospect of corporate employment with the students of the sample and with about eight corporate recruiters, it was apparent that the black students' employment expectations differed substantially from those of their white counterparts. The black student did not demand personal fulfillment aside from being able to perform a worthwhile task and receive adequate compensation, although they were sensitive to any attempt to make them the "token" Negro in any department of a company. They did not resent it if the recruiters suggested that they needed additional training either within the firm or in company-sponsored night courses. Several years ago corporate recruiters did not go into this issue squarely and honestly with black students, partly because they were afraid of offending the students and partly because they were only recruiting "token" Negroes for their companies; this has changed in recent years, however, and the black college graduate is generally acknowledged to be a worthwhile employee in his own right by most major corporations. The millennium is not at hand but, as corporate recruiters continue to seek out the black college student, the results are more encouraging.

In the past, perhaps the single greatest obstacle for black students concerning corporate employment was getting over the hurdle of the personnel office. The curious attitude of professional personnel people toward almost anyone seeking employment and the lily-white complexion of most corporation executives caused black students to approach job interviews as if they were marching to the guillotine. This reluctance is no longer so prevalent among black students, but if corporate recruiting among blacks is to be even more effective in the future the professional personnel man's cold hand must be replaced by one that is warm and reassuring. There is no necessity for personnel offices to bend over backward, but if there is value in hiring blacks then there is value in treating them as individuals and with dignity.

Several of the students explained their feelings about a corporate career in terms of both fear of acceptance and fear of failure. They admitted that they were apprehensive of being accepted because they weren't sure whether it was based only on the fact that they were black or on what they actually could do or learn to do; they knew so little about the personal, professional, and technical demands of the corporate world that they were not able to relate their ambitions and abilities fully to those demands. One girl who got a job with one of the prestigious "think tanks" in Washington as their first black research assistant voiced her fears by saying: "It wasn't so much that I was the first black research assistant they ever hired, but more that there was an implied challenge or expectation that I had to be better than the other girls because I was black. I think I can do the job at an acceptable level, but I don't know whether I can or want to carry the responsibility of 'my people' to work every day."

The students rejected the Nixon Administration's "black capitalism" plan on the grounds that it tended to perpetuate the ghetto business conditions it was supposed to eliminate and would merely substitute black for white economic exploitation of the black poor. They agreed that something should be done to eliminate the outrageous business practices directed against black people by those out to make a fast buck, but the idea of black entrepreneurship, even with government backing, did not appeal to them personally. One student, who had spent several summers "interning" with the Small Business Administration, said (and most of those in the sample agreed), "Maybe it's a good thing for a black man to have his own business, but why bother if you can do as well—if not better—for yourself and your family by working for a big company?"

Thus, we can say that the black college student is predisposed to accept Calvin Coolidge's remark that "America's business is business" insofar as they believe in the capacity of business to get things done. Although they are still somewhat uneasy about careers in big business, they are becoming more confident as the major companies are beginning to make their employment practices more "color-blind" and to take steps to remedy some of the black students' academic deficiencies. Finally, their acceptance of the legitimacy of profit in business operations and their understanding of the limitations placed on business by government and organized labor tend to enable the students to counter the black activists' claims about business' lack of social responsibility with a belief that the lot of black people can be improved by a general increase in production rather than through the forced distribution of income. In this regard, almost everyone in the sample was keenly aware of the efforts, problems, and successes of big business. For example, they appreciated the life insurance industry consortium's investment programs in the ghettos, private job-training programs, and the efforts made to allow minority-group employees to overcome many of the barriers posed by trade, professional, and labor organizations in order to obtain meaningful employment.

This point needs to be emphasized, for although the black students have a uniformly negative attitude toward the restrictive practices of trade, professional, and labor groups, they see no need for a head-on confrontation with these organizations on the issue of racist restrictions. The students see America's labor unions as totally irrelevant to their future needs or to the needs of black people in general. Their attitude is not surprising in view of the fact that for every black master electrician in the city of New York there are twenty-five black PhD's. Such extremes in job distribution between blacks and whites are not lost upon the students, who react to union membership—at least in trade unions—with "who needs it?" Thus, the job opportunities opening up for blacks in the white-collar management and technical side of business are seen as a means to bypass the labor unions' control over entry into their trades and perhaps, in the future, to put pressure on the unions' restrictive entry practices from above, not below.

The news media was the next area we probed with the black college students, and their attitudes tell us more about the general lack of communication between blacks and whites than it does about any expectation that the dissemination of information will bring about social change or affect attitudes. If one factor can be isolated, it is that the students feel that none of the news media is able to communicate the similarity in the fundamental goals of blacks and whites. They recognized the particular problems posed for them by institutional racism and the need for the news media to report those problems, but they objected to the tendency to treat them as something unique to blacks. For example, several students were vehement in their denunciation of the press's highlighting of black demands in cases involving protests against malfeasance and fraud where it was made to appear that blackness had more to do with the issues than the facts warranted. One student put it this way: "Hells bells, if the League of Women Voters protests the results of an election it is considered no more newsworthy than 'Dog Bites Man,' but if any group of black citizens does the same thing it is treated as 'Man Bites Dog—Without Being Bitten First.'" They were also particularly upset about TV's attempts to stage incidents for viewers on the ground that such coverage was "good for the black people's cause."

When asked how they would prefer events involving blacks and black organizations to be treated by the news media, they were somewhat inconsistent between pride in their blackness and their desire to avoid publicity that lends credence to the white notion of black "difference." The distinction between black pride and black difference is subtle, but it is very real to the black students and they resent the press's seeming inability to make the distinction clear in its reporting and commentary about racial activities and issues. What this means to the students is that in news reporting there is often an unwarranted conclusion—sometimes implied, but more often stated—that when a black person or organization accomplishes or fails to accomplish some act that this is further evidence of the difference between blacks and whites. Too often, in their minds, the act is judged apart from the motives underlying it, as if it were alien to human beings. As one student said, "Black people cry, hope, and bleed like anyone else, although the press pictures their motivations as not different from those of members of the white race."

In fairness, the students recognized that there had been some improvement in reporting of black accomplishments and failures, but they were not overly sanguine about the ability of the news media to keep black protests in perspective, and almost without exception they believed that the shorthand, condensed approach of the daily press to racial matters only exacerbated relations between blacks and whites. One student who aspired to a career in television believed that eventually in-depth documentary and commentary programs would be of some help in dispelling black stereotypes, although he was pessimistic that there was enough time left for such a long-range process to do any good. When asked why, with these reservations, he planned a career in television, he laughed and said, "I know it sounds inconsistent, but beyond the fact that black TV cameramen are the highest-paid technicians in the U.S. today,* I'd like to see if I could create something of real esthetic value that would reflect the goals and hopes of all men." These idealistic sentiments are yet another expression of the students' belief in the potential of an existing institution that is not completely encumbered by bureaucratism or controlled by men who have closed their minds to the necessity to work for change in American society.

On balance, he and the others were not optimistic about the news media, but they had not abandoned all hope, either.

The students' attitudes about the role of organized white religion roughly paralleled the division of opinion and confusion of purpose which seems to characterize the efforts of various church groups. With only one exception, all the students in the sample had been raised in Christian homes and all were familiar with the Scriptures; however, only 10 per cent considered themselves to be practicing Christians. The students' attitudes about religion are important because even though none of them had

* Black TV cameramen and technicians are in great demand for live-news reporting and documentaries filmed in the ghetto because often they have access where their white counterparts cannot go.

had a direct association with organized white religion, their views reflect an understanding of its ideological relationship to Negro religion.

A common thread in their views was a sense of dissatisfaction with the ability of black and white religious groups to work together on commonly shared goals, whether spiritual or social. Those students who considered themselves fairly religious had an almost nostalgic idea that religion was the one area where integration should be tried even if that concept were abandoned everywhere else. But aside from this minority view, the entire sample rejected—although somewhat reluctantly—a social role for white churches vis-à-vis black people. They revealed a curious mixture of cynicism about the ability of white liberal clergymen and lay leaders to see a problem through to the end and pragmatism about the physical dimensions of the problems, especially in relation to the black poor. For example, they saw the white clergy's early support of the civil rights movement as more symbolic than real or effective. When pressed on this view, because it implied a rejection of white assistance in racial matters, they countered that, as one student explained, "the churches and their liberal followers have real power, and if they really wanted to help their black brothers they should have done it directly, at home, and not waited to join Martin Luther King's freedom marches."

The point is not as obscure as it may seem, because, many students felt, whites can be of more assistance to blacks if, for example, a church director and his board of deacons refuses to hire a contractor who practices job discrimination (organized religion annually spends some $10 billion to $15 billion on church or church-owned construction) than they can by standing in the rain in Mississippi with protesting blacks singing "We Shall Overcome." Examples of other ways in which the power of committed, sympathetic whites could be used both by churches and by the public in general to eliminate institutional racism were cited, but, as the students noted, such actions generate little publicity—and they might cost something.

Thus, the students saw organized religion as almost completely irrelevant to problems involved in social change or helping black people. As one student said, "The church may have its heart in the right place, but its 'frontlash' only ends up on the black man's back after it goes back to doing its own thing."

One final note about organized white religion deserves comment: James Forman's demands for massive financial reparations from America's churches to pay for past unjustices done to black people. The Forman claims and threats, set forth in the so-called "Black Manifesto," will be discussed in Chapter Five, but here it is interesting to note that the students in our sample did not agree with Forman that organized religion is the principal villain in America's racial problem. They recognize quite clearly that Forman has focused on the churches not because of their greater culpability for institutional racism but because they are so badly divided, are so imbued with a moral guilt complex, and are more vulnerable to black pressures than are other institutions.

The final aspect of American society we discussed with the students was the rather general one of culture, or the organic pattern of a society's institutions and practices, in an attempt to identify the students' attitude toward the "American system" in general, or perhaps more properly toward America as a discrete civilization. Since the value of the American system is more than the sum of its institutions, it is worthwhile to see how the black students calculate that value, because, as we have seen, they view some of the institutions as having been pushed beyond the point of usefulness. An underlying theme in our previous discussion has been the students' passiveness vis-à-vis the institutions of white society—that is, the extent that they feel it necessary or pragmatic to seek accommodation with them. The students also are aware of the interaction of those institutions and, more importantly, have opinions as to how they can exert pressure on them to become more socially effective without disturbing their personal accommodation. They know that no world is perfect, and their view of the American system is partially reflected in the question, "Can you live with it?" and partially in a fear of change with unpredictable results and consequences.

"Systems analysis" of this type is in a pre-Copernican state, if it exists at all, and the following views or attitudes are set forth as extremely tentative expressions of what the students think of the overall American institutional structure as a dynamic phenomenon. The questions asked may have been all wrong. Conclusions may have been reached in the ensuing dialogues which may have been inconsistent with the students' fears and sense of accommodation. Nevertheless, the information obtained reveals a latent acceptance of authoritarianism on the students' part and a willingness to undertake—or at least support—some rather drastic actions to bridge the political, social, and economic gap between blacks and whites. Intellectuals —however one may define the term—and liberals with whom I have discussed the students' views have been aghast at the thought of black acceptance of conservative methods to achieve liberal goals, but this is the case in their view of the American system as an *operating* system.

To make our method of examination clear, let us consider how the students feel the system should go about solving a problem primarily affecting black people. Whether such operations are currently feasible or legal is beside the point because we are interested not only in the students' perception of what *is* but of what should be. This is important to remember, because if the students feel strongly enough that institutions are chronically unable to serve as the instruments of change they are not likely to act to preserve or strengthen those institutions.

A problem of some immediacy to black people is the ghetto. Quite literally, millions of words have been written about the ghetto, some scholarly, some polemical, and some philosophical, but very few about how the blacks would solve the ghetto problem if they had control over the necessary political, economic, and social resources—or how they would use power to insure black compliance with their solutions. In general, the black students' answers were forward-looking. They saw the ghetto not merely as the result of one or more phenomena, but also as the cause of these same phenomena, a subtle but important point. In other words, they perceived quite correctly that all elements of a social problem must be dealt with simultaneously, taking into consideration both cause and effect. In their minds, it was just as significant to think of the breakdown of the black family as a cause of the ghetto as to describe it as an effect.

Specifically, their analysis of the ghetto was as follows. The ghetto is a drag on the American system's ability to function properly or effectively. They realized that the so-called cycle of poverty operates to enrich (quietly) a very few at the expense of the many. One student with some background in econometrics described the ghetto in terms of an input-output analysis wherein the inputs from the institutions in both informational form (laws, regulations, and orders) and physical form (money, narcotics, and services) are transformed into the outputs of bad housing, bad schooling, bad jobs, family breakdown, and crime for the ghetto residents and profits to those who provide the inputs. He added that to the extent that black people engage in boycotts directed at system inputs they are involved in an economic revolution; to the extent that activities are focused on system outputs they are involved in a political revolution; and to the extent that they are engaged in changing the implicit rules governing system operations they are involved in a cultural revolution. Others offered their views concerning the relationship between these inputs and outputs, and stated that the implicit and explicit rules governing them were fundamentally in error and needed to be changed, as did the inputs and outputs themselves.

A specific example of reform was offered by one student in relation to the "input" of a rule requiring a certain performance standards for a child in a ghetto school, such as meeting reading-test criteria for promotion. The rule should include mandatory night remedial training for the student if he failed the test, with at least one parent in attendance to insure proper behavior and attention, for as long as it took for the child to perform satisfactorily. Furthermore, the rule itself was not to be arbitrarily handed down, but should be the result of an agreement between a majority of the parents and the school board (locally elected and composed of parents, teachers, and school administrators). If a parent did not accept the majority's decision then the student would not be permitted to attend the school; he could attend elsewhere, but he could not attend that school if his parents were unwilling to abide by the majority's decision.

This kind of solution might be disputed on pedagogical or administrative grounds, but what is important is that the student recognized the institutional change implied in his solution, and most of the other students agreed with the underlying philosophy of the solution. They felt that ghetto education must be improved so that blacks would, in later life, have the freedom of choice afforded by the ability to read as well as white children from suburban schools, and they felt that the end justified demanding increased efforts and cooperation from the ghetto students and their parents. When it was pointed out that the eventual freedom of choice they sought for the ghetto children involved the sacrifice of some freedom now, their reply was straightforward: "To get a little you have to give a little."

In addition, they believed that their provision of genuine local control was a sufficient guarantee of due process to prevent tyranny by a know-nothing minority. One student with a sound background in political theory also contended that "the weakness of democracy's potential for tyranny by the majority is of much less consequence to black people if they are permitted the right to their own 'tyrannizing.' " Their response to the argument that the method of local control of education they were suggesting would result in anarchy and even lower standards in ghetto schools was, first, that black parents *did* want a good education for their children and would not destroy the means to get it, and, second, that because the parents and their children had lost confidence in the ability of the centralized white-dominated boards of education to provide a good education, the parents would accept the responsibility for standards and execution of a local community-determined program. Also, they felt that it was absolutely necessary for the parents to reclaim the schools' right to *loco parentis* in order to maintain discipline and to help stop the dangerous traffic in narcotics. Perhaps the black students' expectations are too high, but as one student asserted: "Mothers of black ghetto kids are much more able and a hell of a lot less intimidated in keeping theirs and other people's kids in line than either the teachers or cops, and if community control of schools can be made a working reality there are many 'welfare mothers' who would be ready, willing, and able to make it work well."

The black students' views on ghetto education have been given in some detail because they illustrate, albeit indirectly, the students' perception of the American institutional system as a working process. They do not want to abandon the democratic process in selecting a course of action, but they do insist that anyone not willing to accept the majority's decision should not participate in the benefits. They also reject centralized government in favor of local autonomy on matters directly affecting the people and external authoritarianism in determining the inputs of the system, although they do not reject the use of outside assistance—if requested by the local governing body—to help solve some of the technical problems associated with education and such other matters as housing and business practices.

In a more general sense, they seem to have little faith in the responsiveness of America's institutions to human need, and they appear willing to sacrifice some "efficiency" in order to make those institutions more responsive. And finally, in an American system which lays claim to the golden mean between anarchy and dictatorship, the only "freedom" of the individual they see is the freedom to say "yes." Although they do not feel that all the institutions of the American system can be effective in solving society's problems, they do not reject the help of any which *do* possess the capability, so long as their assistance is subject to public checks and balances among the people affected and not left to the discretion of the establishment's faceless, nameless elite.

Lest the reader conclude that the black students' advocacy of local control and direction of education is a confirmation of the racist idea that black people seek anarchy rather than education, several points require emphasis. First, the students feel that local control on an autonomous basis should exist only where black people are directly affected *and* are able to control and direct the operation with local resources. Second, they acknowledge that as actions affecting black people directly increase in complexity and scope it will be necessary to accept competent external assistance in those projects, but only as a partner and not as a passive receiver. In this regard, the black students saw the failure of urban renewal, for example, not so much as a failure in planning, but as a failure to involve the black people before the fact and to continue to communicate with them throughout the life of a project. One student put it succinctly: "If Mister Charlie really wants to find out if blacks are unable or unwilling to take care of quality housing, just let him build one project *with* blacks and not *for* them!"

The results of our institutional attitude survey are far from conclusive or complete, but they do reveal a broad spectrum of responses ranging from hostility to indifference to neutrality to acceptance. Both revolutionary and counterrevolutionary space exist within this spectrum, and because personal institutional support, no matter how it is articulated or manifested, is fundamental to maintain any political or economic system, it is essential that we accept the black students' attitudes as a point of departure and as a means as well as a challenge to gain their further support for the entire system.

FIVE

Revolutionary Radicalization of the Black College Student

To say that black college students, as a group, are ready to run amok if all of society's racial problems are not solved is absurd. Since each student has his or her own personal boiling point, it is impossible to predict exactly what would set off one student or a group of students. However, certain sources of heat can be established as being more potentially effective than others in the radicalization process, and thus it is worthwhile to identify those areas that are especially rankling to the black students.

The term "radicalization" is used to mean the actual emotional and physical commitment to and support of revolutionary violence to overthrow the existing government—the political, social, economic, and educational institutions of a country—and to replace establishment leaders with leaders from the revolutionary groups' own ranks.*

---

* As a reminder to the reader, I am using the following definitions: a "militant" is anyone who is impatient with the rate of social change and the elimination of racism; an "activist" is anyone committed to protest and disruptive action to achieve his goals; an "activist revolutionary" is anyone about whom there is insufficient evidence to characterize as revolutionary although he may be considered potentially revolutionary; and a "revolutionary" is anyone who has clearly demonstrated—both by word and deed —that he is committed to protracted guerrilla-like warfare and violent

Implicit in our definition is the almost complete reversal of the behavior pattern of a person who was previously either committed to or tacitly supported the existing institutions. To radicalize such a person is not immediately within the capability of the revolutionary activists because the process is so personal, almost like a religious transformation. However, revolutionary activists can influence or speed up the process by bringing certain information to the attention of the potential recruit, or they can directly or indirectly use fear, hate, and the distortion of truth to produce positive, albeit destructive, behavior. And it is also possible that societal conditions can become so intolerable and frustrating that radicalization could take place without the added pressures from the revolutionary activists.

An instructive example of the radicalization of students is that of the Chinese students during the Sino-Japanese war, which began in 1937, before the United States and Japan faced each other in World War II. The students had been extremely apathetic in regard to the Sino-Japanese war, but as the Japanese tightened their control over the parts of China they had conquered, they were determined to convert the Chinese into Japanese, and they interfered more and more with the Chinese students. The students' gradual disenchantment with the Japanese was not based on ideology but on a conception of their own self-interest, and finally—in what must be considered one of the great turnabouts of history—they organized to petition and demand that Chiang Kai-shek actively oppose the Japanese. Chiang must have been astounded, but he could do nothing to placate the students, since he was committed to a waiting game, as he believed it was only a matter of time until the United States and Japan would collide.*

In the face of this rejection, their frustration growing, the students began trooping off to join the only people promising to fight the Japanese—Mao Tse-tung and his Communists, a rag-

---

overthrow of the government to achieve his goals, although at times, for tactical reasons, it may be expedient for him to assume an activist guise or to infiltrate white-establishment institutions as a completely conformist member of society.

  * See *China's Destiny*, Chiang Kai-shek's famous textbook written for the Kuomintang indoctrination purposes in 1943.

tag group hiding out in the enemy's backyard after being all but completely annihilated by Chiang's forces in the 1927–36 Chinese civil war. Mao welcomed these recruits, and during World War II their potential for leadership was developed in Mao's rearguard holding action (a not-particularly-aggressive guerrilla warfare). They subsequently were used to organize and lead the mass armies raised by Mao after the war to defeat the Nationalist Chinese and gain control of China. And it would appear that revolutionary radicalization produces a relatively permanent transformation, because those notoriously apathetic students who joined the Communists in the late 1930s and early 1940s are today the leaders of the single most repressive dictatorship of modern times.

In China, a very small minority—the Chinese Communist Party and the People's Liberation Army, numbering at most about 4 million out of a population of some 800 million—effectively engineered the complete takeover of a vast nation, literally starting from scratch. Therefore, the following generalizations about the revolutionary potential of black college students should not be discounted solely on the basis of preconceived notions about self-centered students or "good Negroes" or their small numbers. Old rules apply only until they are broken, and we are going to see how the black college students might be pushed to break the rules.

There is one characteristic of the middle-class black students as a group which should be noted before we look at the various areas of pressure and response that might produce radicalization: they are not immediately likely to respond to pressure brought to bear against other blacks unless it directly involves the students' personal well-being or survival. The black activists see this attitude as a "sell out to whitey" and complain about their brothers' lack of soul. Yet this conservatism—which manifests itself in an "I can go it alone, make it in white society, and retain my individuality" philosophy—is increasingly being subjected to a drumfire of propaganda from the right and the left to heighten a sense of blackness/difference and to promote a natural sense of empathy with all members of the black race.

In general, the development of black pride is a good thing, but it could conceivably develop into black racism. (That is why, incidentally, black studies should not be denounced as a threat to the "American way," which tends to scare off the responsible black educators who can make such programs useful and worthwhile, thus leaving the field to whomever may emerge as the black Goebbels.) Also, as the white-black polarization continues, it becomes more and more difficult for the black students to retain their individualistic outlook. Out of self-interest, like the Chinese laundryman who painted "Me Colored Too!" on his store window during the Detroit rioting, they may be compelled to become full-fledged soul brothers.

The first of the pressure-and-response areas we will discuss is the one that most students feel is potentially the most likely to produce radicalization: so-called police brutality, police overreaction to ghetto crime and rioting, and the police acting more in a political role than in a strictly law-enforcement role.

While the students do not accept the activists' claim that the police are engaged in a systematic attempt to kill off all blacks, neither do they have an image of the policeman as a friend and protector, in spite of extensive efforts by various metropolitan police human-relations departments. Without exception, the students I spoke to had either had a personal experience or direct knowledge of police excesses, and they felt these excesses were completely unjustifiable. They realized that the police are required to act to defend themselves or if there is obviously "clear and present danger" to anyone's life, but they felt that the police have taken it upon themselves—with the encouragement of white society—to *eliminate* protest rather than merely to *prevent* trouble once protests are begun. The question is not merely one of degree; it goes to the heart of the matter. A democratic society, by definition, does not possess the right— that is, the consent of the governed—to use pre-emptive violence, even in a case involving national survival, to maintain the sanctity of one of its institutions. If the police are unable or unwilling to uphold the principle of due process, the black students feel no obligation to turn the other cheek.

In discussing how they would react as individuals to police excess directed against them personally, the consensus seemed to be: to fall back initially, think it over, and—if they were angry enough—counterattack in the most effective manner possible. When asked if this meant they would resort to equal or greater excess to redress the personal wrongs done to them by the police, they reluctantly said yes. In one sense this represents a form of fatalism because it would show that the students had given up hope that police excesses could be met with anything but violence. An attitude of fatalism in black students, among whom there is an almost unbounded zest for life, is perhaps the highest price we could pay to tacitly continue to condone police excess to maintain "law and order."

The students' feelings about police excess reflected their awareness of a class—not ethnic—basis of police hostility; that is, they felt that the police were unfair to disadvantaged persons in general, not only to blacks. In this view, they perceived a relatively obscure historical truth, which is that America is the first and only democratic society to derive the overwhelming bulk of its policemen from the same socioeconomic class from which a large percentage of society's criminals are spawned. This is not to say, of course, that there is a "criminal class," but the students' point is well taken because there is little doubt that environment, in its total meaning, does have a marked effect on subsequent personal behavior, attitudes, and responses. One student, for example, said of the police riot in Chicago at the Democratic convention: "You know, when I was looking at the faces of those cops while they were clubbing those kids, I wondered what happened in their lives when they were growing up." It remains for sociologists to answer his question, but if the students are right in sensing a class bias in police organization, then the police are more likely to be inclined toward pre-emptive elimination of real as well as imagined challenges to America's institutional system rather than toward the protection of the rights of those raising the challenges.

The students were not being accusatory nor were they engaging in idle recriminations against the class bias in police forces; they were more concerned with the result that such bias produces. They could see the police's dilemma in dealing, on the one hand, with persons who had no hope and, on the other, of fearing that their own relative position in society's pecking order would be imperiled if the causes of crime were eliminated.

For after all, the question is not only "Who wants to be a cop?" but "Would we need as *many* cops if most of the causes of crime were eliminated?" The students' view that the police were a threat both to them as blacks on the way up and to society in general reflects their keen awareness of the gulf between the fact and the promise of "law and order." The dichotomy between the unchecked crime that victimizes everyone in the ghetto and the massive police actions taken against those who in rage and frustration lash out primarily against one another is a source of concern to the black students, even though they know they have little power to resolve it.

Finally, the black students totally rejected any attempt to politicize the police—that is, to use the police to preserve any political group, whether elected or appointed. They feel that there is a definite, categorical difference between Mayor Daley's Police Force and the City of Chicago's Police Force—and the former is anathema to them. The students recognized the line between protest *qua* protest and disruption for disruption's sake in seeking the redress of grievances from duly constituted authority, but they rejected the police's right or authority to prevent protest which, by definition, is designed to be disruptive. Disruptive protest can generate a lot of antagonisms and bring submerged feelings to the surface. In the long run this can be beneficial, but only if, as the students insist, the police act as a referee and not as a participant with a stake in the outcome. The term police interference is not nearly as evocative as police brutality, but it may be more revolutionary in its implications.

Thus we may conclude that police excess, brutality, interference, or punitive actions taken against blacks in general are not enough in themselves to radicalize the students, although they do cause anguished concern. But if the police act improperly against the black students themselves, it is much more likely to push them to the point of radicalization.

To anticipate briefly our discussion of the role of the black activists in the black students' radicalization process, the students are quite aware that the activists would like to goad the police into punitive actions and that they try to confuse illusion and reality by inducing the police to act on the basis of what they anticipate the facts *should be* rather than what rational examination shows them *to be*. The students completely reject this tactic as being in no one's interests but the black activists', but they are equally adamant in rejecting a nondiscriminatory police response ostensibly aimed at the black activists but in which innocent bystanders get clobbered. One student said, "All cats may be gray in the dark, but if the police shoot at *this* cat's eyes just because they happen to be watching the police do their thing, they'd better look out because I'll shoot back." The black students speak not the ancient doctrine of Nemesis, "who keeps watch in the universe and lets no offense go unchastised," but rather reluctantly the doctrine of survival, to "do unto others what they would do unto you."

The next area of pressure and response that could influence the black student's radicalization is the withdrawal or loss of a *filled* expectation. It can be one of a political, economic, or social nature, but its relevance to the process of radicalization is that it had become an integral, accepted part of the individual's life. For example, the personal trauma of losing the economic security supplied by a meaningful job is much greater for someone who has worked long and hard to achieve it than for someone who has done little or nothing to achieve a similar position, because the latter person has not had the preceding period of struggle and fear in getting the job. Each black American's personal gain represents a hard-won battle and will be tenaciously defended. In short, the black American will not accept the doctrine of "strategic withdrawal" once he has been able to secure a personal objective, but this should not be confused with the blacks' method of achieving their goals, which often consists of "two steps forward, one step back."

To clarify our discussion about the loss of filled expectations we must expand our earlier definition of black student militancy to account for the phenomenon of filled expectations and its effects. Not only are nearly all black students impatient with the rate of social change and the artificial barriers to their development because of institutional racism, but they are even more impatient with social, political, and economic regression and are willing to participate in disruptive activity to prevent such regression. In other words, the rhetoric of America's institutions may be much more explosive, as far as the black students are concerned, when the dollar and political costs of carrying out the promises made in such legislation as the Employment Act of 1946 or the Civil Rights Act of 1964 cannot be paid.

We must stop thinking that the positive is of paramount importance in racial matters. In reality, the avoidance of the negative is of equal—and in many cases greater—importance. Before we deal in specifics, a few general cases may be cited to make the point clear. For example, following the assassination of Martin Luther King, blacks as a whole "turned off" the Johnson Administration's efforts to assist them; programs that made promises to black people lost their appeal, and the goal of interracial cooperation was downgraded. And all this—and more—occurred at a time when a greater, not less, degree of amity was required between blacks and whites. Yet we have still not learned the lesson of Martin Luther King's death and its riotous aftermath: that is, that black Americans are no longer willing to accept an action, if it is personally and socially regressive, on the basis of what was done *for* them yesterday.

The Class of 1970 is the first group of black college graduates whose entire educational experience has ostensibly been derived under conditions outlawing school segregation solely on the basis of race. They have no illusions about their educational experience, and they are not convinced of the value or necessity for further desegregation, but insofar as it was a gain won at considerable effort they oppose any legal or extralegal maneuvers to take it away. In this regard, the only significant polarity or antagonism, as opposed to indifference, that black students have manifested toward President Nixon was based on his apparent support, in June 1969, of Senator Strom Thurmond against Secretary of Health, Education, and Welfare Robert Finch when Thurmond attempted to get Finch to "go slow" in withholding federal funds to South Carolina's segregated school districts because of their failure to comply fully with the provisions of the Federal Aid to Education Act. Although none of the students in our sample had a direct connection with the areas concerned, they were all opposed to Thurmond's alleged interference. As one student said, "The Man said he was going to carry out the law for all people, and if he lets Thurmond make use of his [the President's] power to stop the law for black people in South Carolina, I may be next in New Jersey."

Thus, in the area of political negativism or regression, the connection between the student and the act itself does not have to be direct to evoke a hostile response. However, the reverse does not hold true, because the same students viewed new and additional proposals for similar and related purposes with indifference, almost as if they felt the government was wasting its time trying to do more when it couldn't do the jobs it was already committed to. Unfortunately, this problem is only dimly recognized, if at all, by President Nixon's band of social reformers, who seem convinced, according to the black students, that the way to keep the black community cool is to dazzle it with their footwork by introducing more new programs instead of striving to make the old ones—and the old laws—work.

The political aspect of pressure and response in the black students' radicalization seems to be less volatile than the economic aspect, although the two areas tend to reinforce each other when they overlap. We have already seen that the black students are positively motivated with respect to earning a living and achieving a reasonable degree of financial and economic security, and that they prefer to accept worthwhile adequately compensated employment with a going concern rather than become innovative entrepreneurs. They are neither black nor white in this regard, in that they would accept or reject employment with a predominantly or exclusively white—or black —company. In short, they are willing and anxious to work and a bit cautious about tokenism, although not so much that they are unable to distinguish sincere from insincere attempts to bring them, on the basis of their merits, into a company as the first black. But because in the past *many* blacks have been hired by government, business, and industry on a token basis or as compensation for past discrimination, there is a real possibility that firing them, even for justifiable causes, might radicalize them.

To hire one black for every nine whites newly hired *may* be sufficient to prevent the kind of racial confrontation that brought the Eastman Kodak Company in Rochester, New York, to a stop in 1967–68, but when the profit or appropriations picture is colored red, to "release" ten blacks on the grounds of their efficiency in relation to the entire work force, regardless of the level of skill involved, could cause social disintegration of the worst order. As long as the profits and appropriations are going up there is little concern about the performance of the marginal, i.e., the newest, employees. If the new employees are average or above, so much to the good, and even if they aren't, the *new* average only falls slightly, whereas the total profit is greater, although smaller on a *unit* (individual contribution) basis. What makes this point so pressing is that the blacks—and especially the black students—are psychologically and emotionally unwilling to accept their old "last hired, first fired" place in the economic process.

They are opposed to fighting inflation by increasing unemployment because they believe that black people would be affected well out of proportion to their numbers in the total work force. While they are not primarily concerned with those blacks who are less qualified for business than they are, they feel that if relatively unskilled blacks are the first to be let go the process could eventually affect them, too. When government economists talk of a necessary unemployment rate of 6 per cent to reduce inflation, the black students interpret this as a reduction in their job opportunities by as much as 10 to 15 per cent. The problem is real and not easily solved, but there are several steps to take to lessen the potential for radicalization in this area.

The first is to supplement "positive discrimination"—that is, to hire more blacks to correct past racial imbalances—in employment practices by a consistent effort to upgrade the skills of any blacks so hired in order to insulate them from temporary vicissitudes in business conditions. Obviously it is not possible to insulate them from all the ups and downs, but training beyond so-called on-the-job training is necessary to realize the full potential of blacks hired, regardless of their level of skill. Black productive potential must be enhanced so that they can be spread among the work force on a normal distribution basis, and thus be more insulated from what appears to be a racially discriminatory reduction in force at a time of reduced activity. This type of "applied economics" differs from conventional business and industry practices because it aims to make the worker a fully functioning member of a firm, with the responsibility for fulfilling the worker's full potential shared equally by the employer and the employee.

The second step was suggested by the students, who rejected the idea of being "undermatched" with their jobs. They felt that the best way to determine their real potential was to measure the performance of a black employee against that of a white employee with the same qualifications. If the blacks didn't measure up, they should be given the opportunity to close the gap, and if they were unable to do so they should be let go. They felt that being allowed to stay in a job when they were not doing as well as they should be amounted to a disguised paternalism that could only be demeaning and make them resentful and unwilling to do their best. But for the white business and government hierarchy to implement such a program would require a much greater degree of personalization (leadership) at a time when the tendency seems to be the reverse. Furthermore, personalization in the work process is difficult to achieve because the ultimate and elusive variable is man, and neither blacks nor whites may have the energy and character to develop a self-cycling, self-supporting value system based upon free and open intercourse between them.

Finally, the black students were very concerned about what their reactions might be if they were fired as the result of an economic whipsaw and they had been deceived by themselves and their employers as to their actual worth to an organization. As one student said, "If I don't have it, or whitey thinks I don't and honestly tells me so, I can accept that fact; but if he uses me for his own purposes to 'prove' his liberalism I don't know what I might do, but I don't think it would be peaceful." They also feared, although not as much, the self-hate they might feel if they were *not* fired from a job when others of greater ability were let go in their place during an economic squeeze. This, in my opinion, was a healthy sign because it showed that even after 400 years of white racism the carapace around their sensibilities had not become so thick that they rejected equality, or the competition it implies, in favor of a false security purchased with their self-respect.

In sum, they approached their future careers with some trepidation, some confidence, and considerable courage. They see work as part of their personal fulfillment, and perhaps this vision foretells the danger and the promise ahead, because if that personal fulfillment is denied them for causes which can be eliminated, they acknowledge quite openly that their reaction would probably be quite hostile. As we shall see, the actions of the black revolutionaries are designed to play on the black students' fears, misgivings, and uncertainties in this and other areas so that it is nearly impossible for the students to ignore the possibility that future failure might be due to their blackness.

The next area of pressure on the black students is social regression. As we have mentioned earlier, the black students feel that legal and formal acts of political regression are intolerable, but acts of social regression do not especially upset them. Their reaction is interesting because in some ways it seems to confirm the conventional southern white belief that Negroes really prefer to "stay with their own kind." That may be true to some degree, but not for the reasons advanced by white supremacists. Specifically, as the students have developed "black pride" they have come to regard social intercourse with whites on a take-it-or-leave-it, case-by-case basis. In areas where race is not an issue and where sensations, perceptions, and meanings can be shared equally on an interpersonal basis, the black students are indifferent to color. They appreciate various life styles not in terms of possessions, but in terms of the personal value in sharing similar experiences and aspirations. For example, in thinking about where they wanted to live, they were more concerned about whether their neighbors shared similar attitudes and outlooks than whether the neighborhood was integrated or segregated. Even so, they totally rejected the hypocrisy in legal attempts to deny a black person the freedom to choose where he wants to live. Their distinction between social and legally enforced integration, although the one may be the precursor of the other, is perhaps the greatest measure of their maturity in dealing with personal and social problems, for it reflects a willingness to evaluate persons and social actions on an intrinsic, individual basis rather than from an externally derived preconceived position.

There are whites (and blacks) who may see the black students' desire to retain their personal freedom of choice in social matters as a way to shed their blackness or avoid racial confrontations. Neither view is correct. The students are learning to be more proud of their blackness, and are enhancing their personal dignity by keeping their color difference in its proper perspective through a greater appreciation of the worth of the individual. On the other hand, the quiet dignity with which the black students are preparing for life's challenges is a constant affirmation that they would never deny their blackness to achieve a personal sanctuary from racial conflict. One student reflected, "There are many blacks who have bought what they thought was peace and safety by becoming 'white' in their thoughts and actions, but I think black students have seen this to be a bad bargain. Our hope is that in the future such a price won't be necessary to become a real part of American society."

In sum, the black students' social outlook seems to crystallize around two premises. First, social intercourse is a matter of individual conscience, style, and the reciprocity of interests between people. Second, acts of social regression taken by individuals or groups to prevent the black students' freedom of choice would be strenuously resisted, and that if the power of institutions was used to turn back the clock they would be predisposed to support countervailing power, although not directly at first. If America's institutions foster social regression, the black students would provide moral and financial support to those who physically opposed such practices, and if the practices become widespread and self-reinforcing they would probably join with those engaged in forceful opposition.

These potential reactions can be seen as steps in the black students' radicalization, but the process is not that orderly because the revolutionaries are constantly trying to confuse the issues and keep the students from thinking clearly about all the decisions they must make about interpersonal and interracial relationships. With this point in mind, let us turn to the methods used by the black revolutionaries to confuse the black students in their efforts to push them toward a commitment to revolution.

Black college students are subjected almost constantly to black revolutionary propaganda, some of it so superficial that it lacks even a half-truth to make it credible even to those students inclined to believe the worst about "whitey." It is also largely irrelevant, as far as the black students are concerned, because of its tendency to overemphasize the nonimmediate past, that is, the ills of slavery. Even so, much of the propaganda does have an effect on the black students because of its focus on the *hypocrisy* of white society's ideals when compared with the actual results achieved in attempts to implement those ideals.

When we discussed the content of a wide variety of Black Panther and Revolutionary Action Movement literature, several of the students pointed out that it was most effective when it let the white establishment convict itself out of its own mouth. Most of the revolutionary literature took statements about what was going to be done for the Negro and compared them with the actual result, and insisted that the result—good, bad, or indifferent—was not nearly as important as before-the-fact grandiose claims that were designed to "sell" the program to black people. To counteract this the black students felt that the white establishment should use "soft-sell" techniques: introduce genuine new programs or reactivate old programs without fanfare and let actions speak louder than words. They believed that to advertise the nominal, necessary acts of government as "programs for blacks" was hypocritical because they usually were no more than the expected, accepted social services performed in white communities. In the black propaganda war no white gets credit for doing what he should do, and he is blasted by the revolutionaries if he advertises his good intentions to do what he should do and then follows up with an Edsel.

Unfortunately, the white establishment rejects *all* black revolutionary propaganda, seeing it as a threat to the status quo. This is short-sighted because it contains clues as to how to eliminate frictions between blacks and whites before they reach the kindling point. As has already been pointed out, part of the radicalization process is to identify for those who are the victims of a discriminatory practice just what it is that is victimizing them. Thus, black revolutionary propaganda contains the diagnosis that could provide the basis for a pre-emptive social strategy, or at least an answer to the plaintively voiced question: "What *does* the Negro want?" Obviously, the propaganda is designed to tell the black man what he "wants" according to the revolutionaries' own lights, but that doesn't mean it can't be useful in preventing a race revolution.

Another important aspect of black revolutionary propaganda is that it is read widely throughout the black community, and the black campus is part of the community. The students read it because they have to, almost out of a sense of self-preservation. Although they do not yet *actively* support the revolutionaries' cause, their failure to be aware of revolutionary matters is construed as opposition to that cause—that is, "if you aren't with me you're against me." The pressure to take, read, and assimilate the black revolutionary propaganda frequently involves real acts of terror and physical coercion that are effective because the black students have no place to hide while awaiting the passage of man's inhumanity to man. Several students who were strongly motivated both by their ambitions and their home environment to seek a typical middle-class life for themselves confessed that the revolutionary propaganda had prompted them to question those values, made them somewhat angry in an ill-defined way, and caused them to see racial overtones in situations where they knew race was not an issue. A full study of the black students' reaction to propaganda is not feasible at this time because as yet they have neither finally accepted nor rejected the necessity for revolution, but their responses seem similar to those of white Americans who were encouraged to hate the "dirty Hun" on the basis of spurious pictures of the gruesome results of the beheading of Belgian nuns by Kaiser Wilhelm's soldiers before America entered World War I.

Obviously, the best propaganda is based on truth, but with skill and repetition it is possible to get equal, and in some cases better, results with half-truths or lies if the object of the propaganda does not know how to counter it. In this case, the students' feeling that the white establishment should either put up or shut up has considerable merit; as one student said, "It is becoming harder and harder to give the white establishment the benefit of the doubt, and in conversations with the hard-core activists it is much safer not to get caught up in an either/or proposition between what they say and what the white establishment says." He added that it was hard enough to steer a middle course on social issues without endless insistence by whites that protest had to be nonviolent and that progress was being achieved.

But propaganda is not an end in itself. It is only a means to an end: enlisting those persons in the potential revolutionary army whom the revolution's leaders must have to achieve their purpose. No one can say with certainty exactly what the black revolutionaries' ultimate aims are or how far they are willing to go to achieve them, but the black college students believe that the revolutionaries mean precisely what they say when they call for the violent overthrow of America's white-dominated government.

The important point to remember in this propaganda struggle is that it is not being carried out in an abstract way but is a practical problem each student is confronted with every day and which he must solve in his own way. The black students are continually exposed to both overt and subtle black activist and revolutionary agitation that is difficult to live with, especially in regard to their future plans, because it plays on their fear of the unknown. These considerations are most pressing in relation to the recruitment of black college graduates by firms with a past history of discriminatory labor practices at all but the most menial levels. As has already been mentioned, there have been no demonstrations or protests directed at any corporate or government recruiter on any Negro campus, but that doesn't mean there isn't a great deal of activity after the recruiter leaves and the student completes his job interview. Because some firms have a better record than others, the technique is not used against every student who seeks corporate or government employment, but those who are interested in companies whose past record indicates a tendency toward tokenism are treated to a second "interview" by activists or revolutionaries. They raise such questions as: "Why do you think the Man really wants to hire you?" or "How you going to like being the nigger dummy in the window?" or "After they finish using you, just remember we're your only real friends and the only ones who are going to help you." This technique is most subtle and effective because it articulates feelings and raises doubts the students would prefer not to face. Furthermore, these fears are usually heightened by friends, families, teachers, and well-meaning classmates who have their own tales of discrimination to tell and end up by advocating taking a good "safe" job instead of entering "whitey's world." The effects on the black students are insidious because they breed self-doubt and provide a ready-made excuse for failure in "whitey's world" and make refuge in the arms of the revolutionaries seem more appealing and realistic.

The black students' resolution of this problem remains in doubt because to some extent they must rely on whites to help them reach a positive solution, and whites can help by recognizing these students as persons of distinct value in themselves, exclusive of their revolutionary potential. The point is re-emphasized because if the black students are only seen as pawns in a counterrevolutionary game and not as persons with a potential to fulfill their own real capabilities, this attitude is bound to become plain to them and could do as much to radicalize them as the loss of employment.

Potential black revolutionaries do not stop with propaganda and "friendly persuasion" to enlist the students. They sometimes use physical coercion and intimidation on a selective basis, forcing an individual student to participate in an illegal activity and then holding that fact over his head to insure future compliance with revolutionary discipline. Such tactics include doing "favors" for the revolutionaries such as buying weapons for them, storing narcotics and revolutionary paraphernalia, or distributing propaganda.

One student who sought my advice about what to do in the face of revolutionary coercion illustrates the problem. The student, a serious-minded person who believed in his ability to succeed in life, had been approached by members of a revolution-oriented group and asked to buy high-powered handguns such as the .357 Magnum for them. They gave him a list of shops where he could buy the guns and about $5,000 in cash. They needed his help because the student had a fixed address and no police record. (Those are the only requirements, aside from the money, for the purchase of guns in the District of Columbia or nearby Maryland and Virginia.) The purchaser waits a day or two, during which time the shop is expected to verify this information with the police, and then picks up the merchandise.

The student was tormented by his desire not to do anything wrong and his fear of reprisal, because he was sure that if he didn't go along with the request the revolutionaries would, at some later date, kill him. We discussed his problem at considerable length, but the final decision had to be his, for each man must decide where he will stand by himself. He felt that although he did not want to become a part of the black-white confrontation, and didn't believe a confrontation was desirable, necessary, or useful, he wasn't sure that a refusal on his part—a sacrificial gesture—would do anything to forestall it. This was a real problem, the dirt and slime of revolution, not abstract politics. We both knew that neither I nor all of white society's protective mechanisms could protect him from reprisal.

That discussion was our last, because such is the current state of affairs between blacks and whites that he didn't feel free enough to continue our friendship, and I don't know what his final decision was. But several months after our conversations, which ended with my promise to try not to interfere, because he insisted that I shouldn't, he was shot to death. His assailant was subsequently identified and arrested, but the man's connection with the black revolutionary movement remains to be proven.

One might question why the black students allow themselves to be used for purposes which may cause them serious personal difficulties in later life if they are discovered. The answer can be found in the reality that makes up the black student's life. He is caught in a three-way crossfire from, first, those who are so impatient with the rate of social change that they have embraced violence; second, those—both black and white —who are determined to bring about social change in an orderly manner; and, finally, those who are determined to prevent any social change. In such an environment the black student cannot be blamed for trying to stay out of the line of fire, but to do so often requires him to make some rather bad bargains with the devil because, like those persons who refused to testify against Al Capone, he knows that it isn't possible to receive continual protection. He is often forced to seek an accommodation with the revolutionary reality while hoping that "this too shall pass away."

As one student who had formerly been a member of a revolutionary organization put it, "One of these days it's going to be necessary to put the wild ones down with force—and that's going to make even more of them. And until that time there is no sense in me or anyone else who has to live in the black community to give them any offense." Another student noted, disgustedly, "The only difference between the agitators who bother us in college and the kids who used to run the lunch-money shakedown rackets is that the college crowd has the nerve to claim they're doing it for black people." Then he amended his statement to include two other differences: one, that most of the revolutionary agitators on campus weren't students, or only vaguely claimed that they had once been students at Howard or some other Negro school, and, two, that they made little attempt to get any financial support for their activities from the students. Their big pitch was, he said, to get the students "to join this or that group for the 'cause' without saying just what the cause was all about, beyond being against whitey."

Because there are so many potentially revolutionary organizations working among black students there is no way short of a massive infiltration effort to determine which among them is truly revolutionary in its orientation. Sometimes, although not always, a group's revolutionary orientation can be distinguished from its propaganda but, as a general rule, the more widely organized or well-known potentially revolutionary groups such as the Black Panthers do not agitate or recruit actively on campuses. The students contended that they could see a pattern in the various potentially revolutionary organizations' appearance and disappearance: an organization would come into being—literally out of nowhere—propagandize for a brief time, gain some followers, be infiltrated by the local police or the FBI, and then fold up; then the same leaders would start all over again under a new name several months later. The black students compared the revolutionary recruitment techniques on their

campuses to the operations of the farm system in baseball. The
recruiters would "try out" new members and techniques on the
campus and then pass the talent on to a larger outside organization. There may be some validity to this view because students
who are members of such large organizations as the Black
Panthers or Black Muslims do not, as a rule, engage actively in
overt campus activities and are, in fact, among the most serious-minded students to be found on any campus.

The lack of fund-raising activities on campus is unusual in
agitational or revolutionary practice, for these organizations are
usually born in the "red" (no pun intended), and are always in
need of funds. Yet, without exception, the entire sample of students said there had been no concerted attempt by activists or
revolutionaries to raise money among students for their overall
activities. Even more unusual was that these organizations generally seemed to be well financed and their spokesmen well
dressed. Of course, the general state of affluence in this country
may partially account for this, but it does not wholly explain it.

It is not easy to identify the financial backers of potentially
revolutionary organizations because of the nature of their operations, but with what the students of our sample knew either
directly or indirectly and corroborative evidence from other
sources, a broad pattern of financing can be distinguished.

One immediate source of funds arises out of the relatively
recent phenomenon of "black Jews" in the black community.
The term has no religious overtones, but refers to a stereotyped
view of the business practices attributed to Jewish businessmen.
The "black Jews" are recent immigrants primarily from former
British colonies in the Caribbean who have come to the United
States to go into business. Generally, these West Indian immigrants are better prepared from an academic and social standpoint to cope with the economic environment of white America
because they have a better educational background and are
strongly motivated to achieve a middle-class economic status. In
the cities along the United States eastern seaboard, as the white
businessman has been scared out of the ghetto West Indian immigrants have moved in to take his place. Students from several
of the former British colonies estimated that in the major eastern

seaboard cities from Charleston to Boston between two-thirds and three-fourths of the black businesses employing more than twenty-five to fifty persons established in the past three to four years are either directed or controlled by West Indians. These estimates are generally confirmed by data obtained from the Small Business Administration, local departments of licenses and permits, and persons engaged in granting credit to black businesses.

However, this is not necessarily the black capitalism that President Nixon has advocated. The students contend that the "black Jew's" business practices make those of the white businessmen in the ghetto seem benevolent in comparison. As one student put it: "They've put the sweatshop back in style. They hire the welfare folks who must have extra money, and they have more tricks than a magician to beat the government out of taxes and Social Security withholding." They are specialists in the so-called "No W-2" * job, which enables them to hire a person without reporting the job to the Internal Revenue Service; the employee, therefore, does not pay income taxes but can still collect welfare. According to the students, the "No W-2" practices are widespread and may be found in such service areas as carpet installations, taxicabs, and laundries owned by West Indians. However, because they are operating outside the law, albeit with the explicit and implicit support of the people they hire, they are vulnerable to pressure applied by indigenous "black cause" organizations; money is thus made available to activist/revolutionary groups from the "black Jews."

A second source of black revolutionary financing, of either their own activities or "agitprop" front organizations, is the traffic in guns and narcotics involving black servicemen and black activist revolutionary organizations. There is big money in this operation, which involves the traffic of military weapons from military bases both within the United States and overseas to the major metropolitan centers, where they are engaged for

* A "No W-2" job is one in which the employee receives his pay directly from the employer almost like an independent contractor receives his compensation for services rendered rather than as a wage or salary subject to withholding taxes and social security. The technique is quite simple and most effective for dealing with persons who do not want to report such income.

money or narcotics. If the weapons are exchanged for narcotics the drugs find their way to stateside military bases, where it is now almost as easy to buy narcotics as a cup of coffee.

In the past two years the number of those selling and buying drugs in metropolitan centers and military bases has increased at a rapid rate, and the new generation of drug sellers and buyers seems to concentrate on young people and often ties drug and sales to a black political ideology. In one military base after another strident calls of "black power" have been accompanied by weapons thefts and increased narcotics activity. A causal relationship among these phenomena cannot be immediately proved, but there is a growing conviction among those who must deal with all three problems that there is a direct connection.

For example, at the large Marine base at Camp Lejeune, North Carolina, the unexplained loss of weapons reached such proportions by mid-1969 that Marines were no longer permitted to retain personal custody of their rifles but instead had to sign them in and out on a daily basis. This is an unheard-of practice in the service where a Marine gets to know his rifle so well it is referred to as "she," but one made necessary by the thefts both of individual weapons and of those stored in unit armories, and it coincided with a rise of black activism in the Marine Corps which surfaced in June 1969 when a white Marine was murdered by a mob of black Marines at Camp Lejeune. It is presumed by some military authorities that the stolen weapons are being sold for money or exchanged for narcotics because of the "cash and carry" basis of the narcotics traffic and the expansion of that traffic directly linked to black servicemen.

The traffic in narcotics and weapons thefts is a servicewide problem, but the black serviceman is more suspect in this matter than his white counterpart because of his more apparent connection with the ghetto community and his vulnerability to black revolutionary pressure. Unfortunately for the great majority of black servicemen, who are innocent of any wrongdoing, it is becoming increasingly difficult for military leaders, at any rank, to eliminate either of these problems without creating additional racial incidents like the one at Camp Lejeune or to endanger innocent black servicemen.

Although the domestic traffic in weapons and drugs is severe, the problem is made even more complicated by the illegal insertion of both weapons and narcotics into the United States from military personnel overseas. Military postal authorities estimate that in the past two years the resale dollar value of illegal contraband such as explosives, drugs, and weapons mailed or shipped successfully without detection to the United States—from Vietnam alone—is in excess of several hundred millions of dollars. The temptation is great, because the young serviceman knows that if he can get some of these items back to the states they can be converted into a tidy sum, and he also knows that even if the package is discovered by postal authorities—which is not likely, since they make only a fluoroscope spot check of one in a hundred packages—there is slight chance that the sender will be prosecuted because the problem is so widespread.

In sum, the countraband traffic of guns, explosives, and narcotics is so pervasive that it cannot be explained solely in terms of personal greed. A more reasonable explanation is that individual servicemen are being used by those who need the actual contraband or the big money such traffic produces after it is resold, and the *most* likely candidates to gain from such traffic are the black revolutionary organizations.

A third, though less obvious source, of black revolutionary financing is the white right wing. Students who had been involved with black activist groups said that extreme right-wing organizations had been and still were willing to provide money —anonymously, of course—to promote black segregation attempts. Such support is not as illogical as it might seem, for it is in the interest of both the radical left and the radical right to intensify the polarization of extremes in a society.

A final source of funds is middle-class Negroes, who are susceptible to intimidation. The black revolutionaries don't expect these people to be part of their army, and consequently they are not adverse to squeezing them for money in support of the cause. Complaints are not often heard from the middle-class Negro about these requests for donations, but the practice is so widespread that, as one student whose parents had been repeatedly solicited for funds from a variety of groups, said, "They [the activist groups] ought to get together and form their own

United Fund; that way they'd get more money, cut down on their overhead, and lower the irritation people like my folks are beginning to feel about what they are doing."

Each of these sources of revolutionary funds is relatively covert in origin; recently the activists have been making overt demands for "reparations" from the nation's organized religions, both Christian and Jewish. These demands are seen as more of the bid for public attention than a serious attempt to gain a major source of additional financing, but any money given under a reparations program has a greater value than its dollar amount because it invests the revolutionary cause with a degree of legitimacy, and it also makes it possible for the revolutionaries to commingle funds from a variety of illegal sources. The ability to commingle funds has the obvious advantage in a nonprofit organization, which is not subject to normal tax and auditing practices, of enabling it to use covertly acquired funds for overt purposes in support of the revolution, i.e., to buy such items as radios, automobiles, and medical supplies and to lease warehouses and buildings.

There is one final feature of the black students' revolutionary radicalization we must consider. Overall, the students have positive goals, but there are many forces, both black and white, to which they are only pawns in a struggle for ultimate power. As this struggle continues the black students are going to be hard-pressed to maintain the legitimacy of their grievances and to distinguish their goals from those who seek either to make mischief or acquire personal power.

The one overriding danger which, in combination with other pressure, could irrevocably radicalize the black college student would be a form of "black McCarthyism" in which dedicated blacks seeking needed, justified change are lumped together with revolutionary radicals seeking destruction of the system. This much broader-based form of white backlash would be the result of intensified white-black polarization in which black hopes and gains would be lost in a stand-off, and this new crop of white supremacists would certainly include many erstwhile white middle-class liberals as well as blue-collar conservatives. The black revolutionaries would lose no opportunity to manipulate this polarization for their own ends, to push for the devastating confrontation that is their goal.

These voices would drown out the students' simple statement—"I am a man"—with cries of "Put the Negro back in his place!" If this happens, the black student will have no alternative other than to join the revolutionaries to make a last stand for his dignity and self-respect. We would be at that point of no return described by Emerson: "My neighbor feels the wrong; he shrinks from me as far as I have shrunk from him; his eyes no longer seek mine; there is war between us; there is hate in him and fear in me."

This need not happen, but every action and reaction of black and white intransigence heightens our fears and ominously reminds us of the fragility of the bonds of tolerance that bind us together. And once those bonds are broken, reason is no match for prejudice. This, then, is the final futility and frustration for the black college student—indeed, for all who believe in a society of reason.

SIX

Methods and Tactics of the Black Revolution

THE BLACK REVOLUTION is upon us and it won't go away just because we ignore it or refuse to believe that its spokesmen mean what they say. History records societies which have ignored the telltale signs of rebellion and have perished. Perhaps we shall do the same, but on the hope that a dry-run black revolution will prompt us to take action, the following partial scenario showing how the black revolutionaries will be able to win is offered.

As suggested in the previous chapter, the black college students' potential for radicalization varies in relation to their degree of hostility to society's institutions, but the black revolutionaries' ultimate method of radicalizing even the most nonhostile students is the initiation of revolutionary violence. This is important to understand; if the revolutionaries can finally radicalize the students, the chances of the revolution's success are greatly enhanced because the students will be the agents to continue to expand the struggle beyond the scope of the ability of the keepers of the status quo to contain and destroy it. Thus, throughout the scenario keep in mind the fact that black revolutionary violence is not violence for violence's sake alone, but rather an advertising technique conceived by the revolutionaries as the means to get the "salesmen" they need to put the revolution across on a national basis. Furthermore, revolutionary reasoning is such that once the preconditions for revolution exist there is an almost compulsive urge to start the entire process. The potential revolutionaries believe that these preconditions already exist.

There is a tendency among the tolerant white middle class to recognize that revolution is an infinitely serious business but to dismiss the likelihood of its occurrence. However, these pressures are not evenly distributed throughout our multipolarized society, and while both the white middle class and the lower-middle-class first- and second-generation Americans may still believe that the U.S. establishment is stable, flexible, and open to all qualified newcomers regardless of class or ethnic background, the black minority does not share this view. This is the fundamental contradiction between black and white, but it does not end with an agreement to disagree. Those blacks who feel that violent confrontation is the only way to resolve the contradiction are influential beyond their numbers, and they *are* capable of fomenting a revolution.

The most radical blacks have clearly indicated their intentions in this regard, even though white America finds this outlook hard to recognize and accept. It is true that in some respects the black revolutionary rhetoric reflects the spirit of the romantic anarchists of the nineteenth century, but in others it is fundamentally different. It is based on a vision of hate coupled with one of power, and it has a corrosive and hypnotic effect in the black community. Furthermore, these potential revolutionaries feel, based on their assumptions of American society's brittleness, that the conditions conducive to revolution are at hand. Perhaps their assumptions are not valid, but whether they are or not may be only a matter of degree; the fabric of American society is not infinitely stretchable. From the White House down to the lowliest political leaders our institutional voices have disparaged and deplored the use of violence, yet the fact remains that with the ever-more-emotional action and reaction involved in social protest people can come to accept violence, then to expect it, and sometimes even to enjoy it. And the belief that violence will not accomplish anything is not even shared by all status quo leaders—witness Governor Reagan of California and Mayor Daley of Chicago—much less by such influential black activist leaders as Stokely Carmichael, who has said, "We believe in violence. I am using all the money I can raise to buy arms. It is now necessary to attack police stations and kill policemen."

Before we get into the actual scenario, it is necessary to discuss the matter of infiltration, because many readers may wonder why the revolution can't be nipped in the bud by agents of the local police or the FBI who have joined the potentially revolutionary groups, and why they can't prevent the revolutionaries' plans from being carried out.

Middle-class whites are reassured by the thought that all is right in Christendom because God is in His heaven and J. Edgar Hoover heads the FBI. Perhaps God still has the ability to prevent infiltration of His kingdom as well as to infiltrate the devil's, but Mr. Hoover lacks the power of the Almighty. This is not to say that the FBI and a few sophisticated local police forces, such as Los Angeles', aren't trying, but rather that it is extremely difficult to penetrate a revolutionary organization. Early in its existence, a revolutionary organization is composed almost exclusively of a tightly knit "band of brothers." At this stage there is no question of members' loyalty because they all know one another. As the organization grows, it becomes more difficult to vouch completely for each new member's loyalty, but there are a variety of techniques available to minimize the risk of infiltration, techniques that are generally not used by a democratic society's security organizations. As a case in point, the Fruit of Islam, which serves as the Black Muslim's internal-security arm, is a law unto itself with substantive summary powers, as evidenced by slayings of wayward Black Muslim leaders that bear all the characteristics of gangland justice.* The point is that although it may be possible for the FBI, for example, to infiltrate one or two potential revolutionary organizations, it is most unlikely that agents can be placed in every such organiza-

* See C. Eric Lincoln's *The Black Muslims in America* (Boston: Beacon Press, 1961), pp. 199–203.

tion in sufficient strength at a high enough level to prevent acts of terrorism.

Furthermore, the FBI suffers from the fact that it is almost all white at the investigative-agent level as distinct from informers and the like. The FBI's record with respect to previous non-white hiring is no better or worse than that of any federal agency, and it is senseless to moralize about this; nevertheless, because there are so few black agents with experience, the FBI is ill prepared to engage in the infiltration of potential black revolutionary groups except on a very selective basis. For the FBI to be able to infiltrate black groups extensively enough to determine the *real* revolutionary groups, it would have been necessary to place trained agents in deep-cover, indefinitely protracted assignments ten to fifteen years ago. Such was not the case, and unfortunately there is no way to play "catch-up" infiltration. And if the FBI, with its superior training techniques and infiltration orientation, is unprepared, the situations in the great majority of local police forces is even worse.

Infiltration of revolutionary groups becomes more feasible after they reach a certain critical size and can be more easily distinguished from front or purely activist organizations. But even at this stage infiltration is not a guaranteed success, because then the status quo internal-security forces would have to substantially increase their infiltration programs and as the number of agents is increased the probability of double agents increases proportionally. This problem is common to all intelligence operations and is more severe in relation to a black revolution because the population from whom the agents can be drawn is only one-tenth the size of the population to be protected.

Another problem with infiltration is the "lack of identity" that is prevalent in the black community. In these days of mailing lists, credit cards, Social Security numbers, and the like, many white middle-class Americans feel that the ultimate in privacy is not to be on *anyone's* list of names, government or otherwise. Such anonymity, however, is relatively common in the black community. Black children's births often go unreported, and the Census Bureau admits that there is a significant discrepancy between their population records and the actual number of persons living in the ghettos. Thus there are more opportunities for black revolutionaries to assume "covers," without any fear of detection, than there are for the average white, and they have a relatively free hand in creating identities for their recruits to use in infiltrating white internal-security organizations.

The lack of a suitable birth certificate for the newly created "identity" is no deterrent for the blacks because photostats of baptismal certificates are acceptable substitutes to the internal-security organizations as well as certification by neighbors in the event that birth records are said to have been destroyed by fire, for example. (This point has considerable significance in creating identities, as the Soviets have known for years, because of the hundreds of courthouse fires which have occurred in this country in the past three decades.) Also, documentation for adult life is not a difficult problem because of the easy access to schools, offices, etc., to further establish an assumed identity. The revolutionaries, on the other hand, have an almost sure-fire method of testing someone they may suspect of being an infiltrator by running his fingerprints through a checking process, perhaps as a result of a staged arrest on a valid charge or through the cooperation of a police official who would seek a "make" on the individual from the FBI. And the FBI is wary of letting local officials know who their double agents are in any given area because it increases the chances of exposure, so there is little they can do to prevent this. It is possible in such a process for someone infiltrating a revolutionary organization to avoid detection, at least initially, but to arrange a sufficiently valid cover for enough infiltrators to do any real harm to the revolutionary organization would require a tremendous effort.

Another aspect of the problem of preventing or neutralizing black revolutionary infiltration into internal-security forces, government offices, and private businesses is the fact that as black terror escalates it will become more difficult to be sure of the loyalty of *any* black employed by those organizations because *all* blacks would be vulnerable to revolutionary intimidation and coercion whether they lived in the ghetto or not. Thus thousands of black file clerks, secretaries, mailroom employees, janitors, maids, chauffeurs, and watchmen would pose a potential threat to any white organization's security and would induce a form of "security paralysis" in a society's institutions. That is, there would be no way to establish the continued loyalty of any black person if at any time they could be intimidated by the black revolutionaries.

This would create a critical situation, because action would be taken to counteract this possibility; the instinct of self-preservation is just as strong in institutions as it is in individuals. The status quo's possible responses range from expanded surveillance and security clearance of black employees or a "buddy system" in which a white employee would be assigned to watch and report on his black colleague to firing blacks or, perhaps, ultimately, the physical restriction of blacks in the ghettos or in detention camps.

The latter alternative may seem too outlandish or physically impractical to be taken seriously, but the history of the U.S. government's "protective incarceration" of some 300,000 Japanese-Americans during World War II tends to refute both assumptions. And even if one feels that the action was justified on the basis that at the time of Pearl Harbor we didn't know what native-born or naturalized Japanese might do if Japan invaded the United States that does not explain why the United States kept the Japanese-Americans behind barbed wire for the entire war, in spite of the fact that after the Battle of the Coral Sea in 1942 there was no doubt that the Japanese threat had passed its high-water mark. Another rationalization for incarceration might be to "protect" black Americans from white extremists who might be inclined to meet a black revolution with one of their own. Perhaps it is true that the sheer physical magnitude of the task of putting 23 million black Americans in detention centers would rule out their use, but there are those both in and out of government who feel the problem is a real threat and who believe that blacks could effectively be kept in the ghettos.

Thus, on balance we can say that infiltration of the many potential black revolutionary groups is more difficult for the established internal-security organizations than vice versa, even though the difficulty does not obviate the necessity of trying. The revolutionaries' greater ability to infiltrate the internal-security forces and other institutions poses additional problems for American society because to prevent infiltration it is essential to resort to repressive and basically undemocratic methods. This dilemma underlines American society's vulnerability to a black revolution, for if society protects its institutions in the face of a determined infiltration effect by native-born black Americans it will only buttress the revolutionaries' claims that the society is racist and repressive and help them recruit the subordinate leaders and followers they need to succeed.

And there is one more overall consideration—what of the seemingly invulnerable array of forces on the side of the establishment, with its trappings of power and sophisticated weaponry? There are the local, state, and federal (FBI) police, with a combined total of about 4 million; the state militia or National Guard, with about half a million; and federal troops—Army, Navy, Marines, and Air Force—with about 3.5 million.

Many ingenious new devices for riot control have been developed in addition to the more conventional local law-enforcement and military weapons, and seemingly all kinds of technology, from the eavesdropping olive in the martini to napalm, can be brought to bear to stamp out a revolution. The following devices for riot control, for example, are only a few of the many now being advertised in professional police magazines: itching powders, chemical-identification sprays, new electronic accessories, water fogs to dampen enthusiasm, floodlights that flicker from three to eighteen cycles per second, wind machines, slippery foam, shock foils for vehicles, and electronic devices to feed back and drown out agitators' speeches. To these marvels of applied science can be added some marvels of applied political science—mass arrests, restricted movement, incarceration, informer networks, manipulated food shortages. And, of course, the marvels of applied military science—massive firepower, full-scale warfare.

The problem is that the "humane" countermeasures may not be effective and the not-so-humane measures bring us face to face with making judgments about actions that have traditionally been considered un-American and undemocratic, to say the least. Not that anybody wishes to be naïve any more about the unavoidability, necessity, and legitimacy of using force—

provided the time and place are right. There is now a whole body of literature dealing with protracted revolutionary conflict, game theories of force, and appropriate levels of violence, and there is an increasing number of harassed law-enforcement officials who speak casually about strategies of conflict and cling light-heartedly to concepts of deterrence before revolutionary activity actually erupts. A knowledge of counterrevolutionary theories may be useful, but the mere existence of a revolutionary movement is not sufficient cause to translate these theories into an actual course of action. In the words of Virgil, "*Graviora quaedam sunt remedia periculis*," or, freely translated, some remedies are worse than the dangers.

But even if we could bring ourselves to use them, would all this weaponry, manpower, superior communications be appropriate and sufficient to control a skillful application of what are primarily the techniques of guerrilla warfare, which is so well suited to nullify the superior technology of the establishment's forces? Would it be enough to control dedicated revolutionaries backed by a fearful and largely radicalized black population even though their firepower consisted only of mail-order guns, army-surplus weapons, Molotov cocktails, arms sent from Vietnam, and whatever more sophisticated weapons they could manage to steal from our inadequately policed National Guard armories? My feeling is no, and in the scenario that follows we will find out why.

The first phase of revolutionary activity consists of a carefully orchestrated and sustained series of random acts of terror that appear motiveless and unconnected but which are designed to disconcert the internal-security forces and keep their response to a minimum. The plan includes "complementary terrorism" that not only keeps the police off balance but is interpreted as a positive benefit by the black community.

Let us take one example. In Harlem uniformed policemen often accompany the rent collectors on their monthly rounds. Let's say that as part of an overall random plan, the revolutionaries carry out a series of seemingly uncoordinated attacks on some of the collectors after the police have been diverted elsewhere. Three things would happen: first, the landlord would find it more and more difficult to get anyone to collect his rents, with or without police protection; second, police administrators would have to decide where their forces should be deployed, and would be reluctant to send them on the rent rounds if they were needed elsewhere (or *might* be needed elsewhere) and if there were a high probability that they would be attacked during their duties; and third, since in the ghetto no one loves a rent collector—or a policeman, for that matter, since both are seen as part of the same oppressive establishment—residents would not cooperate with the police in apprehending the assailants and would tend to believe that these acts were part of the revolutionaries' plan to "liberate" them.

The revolutionaries' use of apparently motiveless or nonspecifically oriented acts of violence is enhanced immeasurably by the technique of random target or action selection from among all available possibilities. Random selection means not establishing a pattern of predictable behavior or action.

Unfortunately, the tremendous revolutionary potential involved in the use of randomness has not been considered carefully enough by those responsible for internal security in the United States (or, one might add, by those who directed our external-security operations in South Vietnam). Even in agencies where the revolutionary randomness has been partially acknowledged as a technique, there is a tendency to believe that information fed into computers will enable internal-security forces to head off trouble before it occurs. Yet this approach is valid only if the revolutionaries act on the basis of their past performance. Computers, systems analysis, game theory, and the like aside, the revolutionary *can* act with relative impunity if he selects his objectives from a random list of numbers keyed to each of his objectives or alternatives. In any given area a list of a hundred or a thousand individual acts of terrorism can be established from which the selection of ten or twenty for a given period of time can be made from a list of random numbers—that is, with the numbers relating to specific acts arranged in columns in no definable order. This method of target selection so completely breaks the chain of past performance that the internal-security forces must either simultaneously cover all the possibilities or wait to act until something has already happened, and either alternative benefits the revolutionaries. In the first case it is impossible to deploy the number of adequately trained and equipped forces necessary to cover all potential trouble spots; in the second case they would not be physically able to arrive at the scene in time unless the terrorists exceed their safe "time on station." But the revolutionaries have all the cards because, since they do not seek to seize and hold a specific objective, they have the freedom to choose the precise moment to begin or end an incident.

There are other advantages to the use of random terror tactics. The first is that the ineptitude of the internal-security forces is graphically revealed for the benefit of potential recruits into the revolutionary army.

In order to win more recruits, however, it is necessary for the revolutionaries to "personalize" their objectives for attack, but in an impersonal manner. This seemingly contradictory statement means that the individuals who make up the "system" are no longer faceless entities, but are individuals who can be killed simply because they are part of the system, whether they are liberal, conservative, reactionary, or middle of the road in outlook.° This is accomplished by using random assassination of establishment leaders. We have seen the confusion and fear that was produced by the assassination of national leaders in the past few years; there would be even greater confusion and wider-spread fear if twenty to twenty-five randomly selected Congressmen or officers in major corporations, for example, were killed.

Thus this technique could lead to the second advantage. In the face of these random assassinations the bureaucracy would be paralyzed because no one would know where the terror would strike next, and no one would be safe because it wouldn't

---

° In this connection, there may be revolutionary significance in the Black Panthers' coloring book for little children, which depicts various members of established society as "pigs" and shows children killing the pigs, evidently in an attempt to condition the children to translate their potential frustration with the system into a willingness to use violence in an impersonal manner against personalized, individual targets. Categories included by the Panthers are the police pig; the avaricious businessman pig, who may be a landlord or store owner; the President pig; the National Guard pig; the "faceless" pig—that is, the person who goes into the streets and tells people to be cool and gets paid for snooping around; and a demagogic politician pig.

make any difference what they did—or didn't—do. It would also certainly provoke a massive reaction against any person or group suspected of the assassinations or of being in any way associated with them, and such a reaction would serve, as we have noted earlier, to radicalize even more of the black population. And of course all of this would greatly exacerbate the black-white polarization process, which would in turn serve to radicalize not only more blacks but whites too.

At the present, it appears—from the nationwide rash of sniper attacks against the police (some 4,000 of them, in medium and large cities)—that the revolutionaries are developing their sense of timing and testing their ability to plan and execute acts of terrorism. So far, no one has been able to connect these attacks with a revolutionary conspiracy, but the continued inability of local law-enforcement agencies to apprehend the snipers seems to indicate that they are more than unplanned individual outbursts.

Another feature of the terror pattern is the simultaneous use of the same techniques against blacks who by virtue of their attitude and orientation are inimical to the revolutionaries' purposes. Attacks in Fort Lauderdale, Hartford, and Camden, New Jersey, for example, seem to be part of such a trend—violence directed toward persons who have sought an accommodation with whites and those establishment officials who have tried to implement joint planning or community-development programs. Violence among blacks within the black community is often not taken very seriously by the white community's security forces, but it may have revolutionary implications if it is directed against black businessmen who by virtue of their position in the community are engaging in dialogue and programs with white leaders in dealing with community problems. These attacks will serve to cut off two-way communication between black and white. Any white person who censures any black man for not standing up to black revolutionary intimidation is being completely unfair, because those black persons are literally carrying the brunt of white America's current black counterrevolutionary efforts. Perhaps, if we can get through the next several years (decades?) we will have gained the wisdom to recognize, as the British did after World War II, that "never have so many owed so much to so few." Unfortunately, some of the blacks speaking quietly of cooperation with whites are being silenced, and those remaining are not being listened to.

There is one more advantage to the use of random acts of terror: the creation of another source of funds to finance revolutionary operations. Regular payments will be made to the revolutionaries by those persons who, for a variety of reasons—the least of which is personal fear—want to carry on their normal business in spite of the revolutionaries' activities. Reports from Delaware, Pennsylvania, New York, and Illinois indicate that painting "Soul" on a shop window during a riot represents more than simple empathy with the black man's cause. For example, reports of the Blackstone Rangers gang preventing destruction in Chicago's ghetto following Martin Luther King's assassination by providing protection—at a fee—were widely circulated in press circles in Chicago and elsewhere, yet nothing was officially reported about it, and the reason is that to expose extortion or terror is to force the police to act. And if they act, there is likely to be more violence, which may be beyond their ability to contain. Yet, if the price of keeping the ghettos cool is to enable the black revolutionaries to expand their organizations and gain additional financing, it may be very high indeed.

Terror is the handmaiden to revolution, but its effectiveness varies from one society to another. Unfortunately, this fact is not very well understood by those who contend that a black revolution will not occur here because it cannot succeed. However, a black revolution can succeed in the United States because terror can be effective here. The high degree of interdependence of the countless elements of American life is at once the strength of the American system (everyone doing his separate job to the best of his ability) and its greatest liability if the system is an object of a revolutionary attack. Our people would have a hard time surviving without the simplest mechanical devices, let alone without the products of our modern production-distribution network. The American system is made up of a network of gears that must all work together if the machine is to run, and it does not take any great perception to realize that some gears are more vulnerable than others to espionage or sabotage.

As an example of our society's extreme vulnerability to revolutionary espionage, in the spring of 1969 an act of chemical "warfare" was carried out in broad daylight in the Pentagon by persons who, although they were employees of the Department of Defense, had no authorization for their "experiment" and were not identified until the report of their actions came to light. The situation involved several technicians of the Army's Chemical Warfare Center at Fort Detrick, Maryland, who came to the Pentagon wearing the familiar green coveralls worn by the General Services Administration custodial employees and carrying what appeared to be a small cannister-type vacuum cleaner. They told the secretaries in one of the offices that they were there to check the air-conditioning, but they were actually conducting a test of the effectiveness of a new cold germ, which they proceeded to pump into the Pentagon's air-circulating system through a ventilator duct. The entire process took less than ten minutes, the Fort Detrick technicians noted the data on their clipboards, replaced the ventilator duct, thanked the secretaries, and left with their miniature air-compressor. The experiment was designed by the Fort Detrick scientists and engineers to see how many people would come down with a cold due to the effects of the new flu type of virus that the air compressor pumped into the air circulating system in a gaseous form. The Fort Detrick experiment illustrates all too clearly the vulnerability of a major government installation to a similar "experiment" which could just be used to pump a virulent organism into the air-conditioning system of the Pentagon or another government building that could incapacitate or kill—in one fell swoop— those who are ultimately responsible for making the government work.

Internal-security forces can be likened to the keepers of the gears who see that nothing blocks their movement and who lubricate them to make sure they turn freely. Thus the internal security forces are the first-line defenders of the system and must be neutralized or destroyed if the black revolutionaries are to achieve their success.

The size, status, skill, training, and responsibilities of the police—in any city of the United States—are clearly inadequate to counter a revolution or revolutionary terror. Regardless of the hundreds of crime-commission reports and studies which have sought to establish the optimum-sized police force for any city, no real effort has been made by elected officials or the general public in any of the major cities to increase the number of their police. We believe in the necessity of an adequate police force, but we are unwilling to pay for it. The point is stressed because while serious crime, by any index, has more than doubled in the past decade, in only one year (1969) during that period did the rate of increase of law-enforcement officers exceed the rate of population increase. The size of a police force is not the only criterion to use in measuring its effectiveness, of course, but from the black revolutionaries' point of view the fewer the police the better, because it is simpler to terrorize 1,000 police officers than 2,000.

Obviously the size, status, skill, and training of police forces are interrelated problems. If the police are to handle black revolutionary terror without provoking a situation in which it is necessary to call in outside help, there must be more men who are accepted and supported by the black community and who are able to absorb the sophisticated training to carry out appropriate counterrevolutionary action. Quite soberly, when one contemplates the problem of black revolutionary terror versus the existing police forces, the odds substantially favor the black revolutionary.

For the black revolutionary to destroy the police in their role as the first-line defenders of society it is necessary first to neutralize them and then to provoke massive police response. Neutralization can best be accomplished by use of the random terror technique already described, whereby the movements of the police in a given area are listed as a possible event. From the total of possible events, fifteen or twenty are randomly selected. After selection each area is thoroughly reconnoitered to determine the police's normal movements in the area and to find a suitable ambush site. The first police targets should be patrolmen walking their beats because there is more chance of success with walking targets and the reaction will be to take the patrolmen off the streets and put them in patrol cars. This benefits the revolutionaries because the ability of the police to observe, detect, and apprehend wrongdoers is neutralized somewhat once they become car-bound.

The exact time of each murder is left up to the men doing the shooting although it should probably be limited to a certain period of time, say seven or ten days. The point is important, because if the revolutionary high command calls for simultaneous executions it would probably evoke a premature massive police response or a summoning of National Guard troops into the area. In many ways this tactic resembles that of a duck hunter waiting in a blind for the best moment to shoot an approaching duck.

The question arises as to how many patrolmen out of a total force must be killed or wounded before the police would retreat to the relative greater safety of patrol cars. As a general rule, it can be estimated that in cities with a population between 150,-000 to 500,000, thirty-five to fifty such murders a month for two months would result in a total shift from foot patrols to roving patrol cars. Then the tactic is continued on a lesser scale to keep the police in patrol cars and to set up the conditions for the next stage in the destruction of the police—that is—staged action to provoke a massive police response.

Success in this phase of the scenario does not assure the victory of the revolutionaries, but it does advance the revolutionary process far enough so that normal methods of dealing with social protest are no longer likely to be used to restore order in the black community. The method to provoke massive police response is simple, effective, and almost foolproof. Overwhelming police response to what may be minor trouble stems from law-enforcement officials' belief in the necessity to head off major trouble by a show of overwhelming force. This has worked in a variety of situations, and in riot-prevention training is called the "pounce" technique.

However, "police pouncing" has an inherent weakness in that the reaction forces are not a single, homogeneous element, but are separate elements which come to the scene of the trouble on separate routes and at staggered times and must "check in to the net" after they reach the trouble area to find out who is in command. Then they either take over their own assigned sector for a sweep of the area or reinforce existing units. During this activity, each unit's rear is exposed, and whereas "shotguns to the front" are suitable for riot prevention or elimination, this tactic is ineffective in a guerrilla action, where a force must be able to fire simultaneously on a 360-degree front. The pounce forces must go where the action is, or threatens, which may lead them into *cul-de-sacs*, narrow defiles, and other areas from which withdrawal is difficult or in which their ability to fire is restricted. Thus, the following sequence of events is suggested:

1. Stage several potential riot-inciting acts, such as a fake shoot-out or fight, in an area that is favorable to an attack of the police's exposed rear and to rapid withdrawal by the black revolutionary elements.

2. Have one of the revolutionaries call in the initial report to the police of the fake incident in order to check the time between the report and the arrival of the police.

3. Note the size of the police response, routes of approach, deployment, armaments, etc.

4. Repeat the process at least three times at different times during the high-crime period—6 P.M. to 2 A.M.—to determine which time will evoke the largest response, which also will determine the period when there are fewer back-up police reserves available.

5. Wait at least three weeks between the staged incident and the actual attack.

6. Procure police uniforms, riot helmets with visors to prevent identification, smoke bombs, automatic weapons, etc.

7. Make several dry-run walk/ride throughs of the operation in order to become completely familiar with sectors of fire, timing, etc.; the best ambushers are those who rehearse on the actual ground to be used.

The actual execution follows from the planning sequence. The incident is staged, the police arrive, a few shots are fired from the crowd—perhaps into a plate-glass window for dramatic effect, the police begin their advance, and the revolutionary "police" arrive on the scene from the rear and proceed to cut down the real police. Simultaneously, from the crowd or from a position on the periphery, a revolutionary sniper shoots a couple of innocent civilians. Under these conditions the real police would have to have the fire discipline of one of the "Emperor's Own" not to cut loose in all directions. When they begin to fire, the revolutionaries throw their smoke bombs and retreat in waiting automobiles via planned withdrawal routes. The operation would take between three and five minutes from the time the revolutionary "police" reached the scene, but it would take the real police hours and perhaps days to restore order and figure out who did what to whom.

Thus, with these kinds of preparations, it becomes rather simple for a force of fifteen or twenty black revolutionaries to kill fifty or sixty police officers, provoke a police riot, create further antagonism in the black community toward the police, and, most importantly, cause the local politicos to shift control over an area's internal security to the next line of defense—the National Guard.

As mentioned in Chapter Four, the almost all-white National Guard is seen by the black college students as the white political establishment's "muscle." In addition, its units have no real ties to the areas in which they are expected to restore or maintain order and, with a few exceptions, they lack the training and leadership to operate effectively in the face of organized resistance or terror. These assertions would be denied by the National Guard's powers-that-be, but they are true nevertheless. Still-unreleased studies made by professionals of the Michigan National Guard's inept performance during the Detroit riots in 1967 indicate that Guardsmen would be in serious trouble if the Salvation Army actively opposed them with drums and tambourines. Since 1967 there has been no meaningful improvement or integration in the National Guard, and in the meantime the challenge of racial violence has increased.

The indiscriminate use of the National Guard to restore or maintain order in racially disturbed areas may be likened to rushing a child who has previously gone into convulsions as the result of a dangerously high fever to the hospital every time its temperature goes up even one degree. Because of past racial violence, society has convulsed once, and now every time there is a rise in the body politic's temperature the National Guard is rushed in because it is believed that the next convulsion will occur at a lower temperature than the previous one. Racial disturbances in local areas that a few years ago would have been handled almost as a matter of routine by the police are now turned over to the National Guard.

With the appearance of the National Guard on the scene of actual or potential racial violence, black revolutionaries can really get down to business. The Guard is not brought in merely to reinforce the existing internal-security forces, but to become part of a joint command with local police and politicians or to take over their authority—and it is entering the situation cold. The black revolutionaries know this, and will exploit the division of authority and the lack of detailed knowledge, information, and intelligence which characterize National Guard operations. The police generally resent the usurpation of their authority by the part-time political soldiers, and one of the ways they express their resentment is to call in sick after Guard troops take over, although, of course, this is not a widely publicized fact. But this is only part of the problem created by calling in the Guard. Others include the resentment of black people, who see curfews and the physical occupation by "whitey's boys" only in the black community. They feel that the Guard is not there so much to protect black people as to restrict their movement, and they feel that the Guard treats *all* blacks as potential rioters. It makes no difference to the black community that the trouble, or potential trouble, is likely to occur in those areas.

But how do the black revolutionaries proceed against the National Guard, with its armed and helmeted troops, jeeps with radios, trucks, and tanks? Isn't that enough to deter even the most rabid black revolutionary? These are incidental to the revolutionaries, because the presence of Guard troops signals the status quo's recognition of the fact that the situation is beyond its capacity to control. And aside from the psychological plus, the revolutionary knows that although the National Guard may *look* formidable it is really quite impotent, as will be demonstrated by a consideration of the course of action which black revolutionaries can undertake.

The physical presence of National Guard troops raises the potential for confusion which does not exist when racial trouble is treated as an *incident* rather than a condition to be controlled. To be specific, at the time of Martin Luther King's assassination, Washington, D.C., was occupied by both National Guard and federal troops and a curfew was established to keep the situation under control. In general, the curfew was effective because most people were so frightened as a result of the burning and looting that they were willing to stay home. However, there were groups of young blacks who defied the curfew and were able to move throughout most of the city. After all the officials got through congratulating each other as to how well Washington's "occupation" was carried out, these curfew violations were forgotten, and the particular tactics which had been used in Washington were generalized as *the* way to occupy American cities in the future. Unfortunately, the conditions underlying this racial confrontation may not be typical of future confrontations, because the assassination of King was not a foreseeable event. But effective revolutionary terror must be planned, and the involvement of the National Guard can be made a part of that planning.

If the assassination of Martin Luther King had been planned by the black revolutionaries as part of a program to get National Guard and/or federal troops to occupy Washington, for example, an additional part of their plan, using only seventy-five men, could have brought the city to a complete standstill, produced enough confusion to mask even the boldest of predatory actions, invited reprisals in the black community and radicalized many black students as well as other uncommitted blacks. Such an action, which could be duplicated simultaneously in any American city, involves turning off the lights and disconnecting all the telephones—that is, a complete blackout. Although this part of the revolutionary plan could be initiated before the arrival of National Guard troops, it is more effective once the troops are in place and have assumed control because it enables the revolutionaries to execute additional acts of terror based on the troops' *known* locations and thus sustain the momentum of the revolution.

To continue using Washington as the example, scattered throughout the city are twelve to fifteen one-story bungalow-type houses which contain the electric-power substations. Each is identifiable by its similar architecture and unchanged window curtains, and each is very vulnerable to planned espionage. Specifically, one satchel charge loaded with explosives thrown into each of these substations can turn off—and keep off for an indefinite period—every light in Washington just as if someone had pulled a master switch.

In the second phase, the massive telephone trunk cables (sealed under mercury pressure in large pipes running through the sewer system), made up of thousands and thousands of pairs of thin copper wire telephone lines, can be fused together into an indistinguishable glob merely by lifting the appropriate manhole cover, climbing down the ladder, and placing a live thermite grenade on top of the pipe. And the revolutionaries would probably have no trouble locating these cables because almost any telephone lineman knows where they are—and how could revolutionary infiltration of the power and telephone companies be prevented?

Once the revolutionaries have succeeded in turning off the lights the effectiveness of the National Guard and other internal-security forces would be substantially decreased at night. Night patrols in a totally dark, unfamiliar city constitute a form of "jungle warfare" well beyond the capacity of the National Guard and perhaps of any security force that is not completely familiar with all the alleys, rooftops, and sewers of a city. Also, it should be noted that the lack of telephone service has a paralyzing effect on those who are not directly affected by the revolutionary terror. For example, during New York City's massive power failure in 1965, people trapped in buildings without transistor radios were reassured only because they could use the phone to make some kind of contact with another human being. It made no difference if the lines were busy, because even the dial tone was a confirmation of the hope that there was still someone "out there."

Psychologists have conducted extensive studies with individuals who have been cut off from all familiar sounds and lights, and the studies reveal that there is an induced state of schizophrenic terror accompanied by a heightened auditory sense which frequently produces a "hearing hallucination" effect. The effects of similar environmental changes on an entire population are unpredictable, but are bound to be bad, especially if there are also other revolutionary activities planned to induce panic and terror. The mere fact that daylight will come is insufficient to preserve a population's equanimity because unless essential services can be restored the next day, the second, third, and all successive nights will produce even greater dread.

There is no need to go into all the specifics concerning "dark nights of terror"—the mind boggles at the almost infinite number of revolutionary activities they would make possible. For example, the revolutionaries would be able to engage in a systematic looting that would dwarf anything we have witnessed in previous riots. And, of course, the "do-it-yourself looters" who seem to come out of the woodwork following any natural disaster would be out in force to add to the confusion and hasten the breakdown of the essential food supply and resupply procedures.

One might contend that only madmen would undertake such activities. Fictional accounts, such as Edwin Corley's *Siege*, which tells of a black liberation army taking over New York City to force the U.S. government to turn over New Jersey to them as a "new black republic nation," seem so fanciful that they can be lightly dismissed. And they should be, because in direct confrontation it is unlikely that any black revolutionary force would be successful. However, black revolution has a different aim than face-to-face confrontation; to be successful the revolutionaries do not have to literally destroy the society and its institutions, but only to set in motion the processes whereby the society will largely destroy itself.

Even though American society would be greatly damaged if four or five of its major cities were simultaneously subjected to "dark nights of terror," it would be necessary for the black revolutionary to make sure that future cooperation between black and white would be impossible by playing out the next-to-last act of the revolutionary scenario: the elimination of the regular armed forces as an effective instrument in the maintenance or restoration of the nation's internal security. The regular armed forces pose a different problem for the revolutionaries than the National Guard because they are better trained, better equipped, and have an adequate command and control system and an independent logistical base. However, the armed forces are still vulnerable to actions within the capabilities of the black revolutionaries to stage or manage.

In anticipation of the possible need for federal forces in local disorders, following the King assassination the Pentagon established a riot command (officially known as the Directorate for Civil Disturbance Planning and Operations) designed to plan for, coordinate, and direct federal troops in some 150 U.S. cities. The command is well staffed, is housed in an elaborate center in the basement of the Pentagon (built at a cost of some $5 to $7 million), and has assembled detailed "target" information on each of the 150 cities.* But all this planning and preparation is based on an after-the-fact insertion of federal troops into a large city—that is, after the situation has deteriorated to the point where the governor or mayor asks the President to take charge. And in such a situation the rules of federally declared martial law obtain. These facts are important because under a presidential proclamation of martial law, the President has the authority—as previously exercised by President Lincoln —to eliminate due process and the writ of habeas corpus and to allow his field commanders to exercise summary justice. All of these steps may, in fact, be necessary, but their content and significance should be appreciated by all those persons—both black and white—who will be forced to accept them. Seen in

* The black revolutionaries may have anticipated the danger to their cause through a premature use of federal troops in the 150 largest cities by shifting their emphasis to smaller towns and cities not covered by the Pentagon contingency plans. Last year (1969), according to Brandeis University's Center for the Study of Violence, there was a marked increase in the percentage of civil disturbances in cities with populations of less than 75,-000, including Cairo, Illinois; Oxford, Lancaster, and Farrell, Pennsylvania; Massillon, Springfield, and Lima, Ohio; Ypsilanti and Ann Arbor, Michigan; Evansville, Indiana; and Lakewood, New Jersey. Local officials generally blamed "outside agitators" for the incidents—which all, incidentally, followed the same pattern (protest, police response, looting, burning, and rioting followed by capitulation to the black demands with scant likelihood of any successful implementation). Although there is no immediate, directly provable connection between the rise of racial violence outside the large cities and a black revolution per se, it is in the black revolutionaries' interest because it can serve as a training ground for future revolutionary leaders as well as a source of recruits who may be expected to want to test their mettle later in the big-city environment.

this light, the arrival of U.S. Marines in New York, Philadelphia, or San Francisco means that the entire population will do what it is told to do—or else.

There is considerable prudence involved in the administration's decision to establish a riot command; however, like the ABM, it can be fully tested only after the event it is designed to deter occurs. Yet, the riot command's deterrent effect is, also like the ABM's, based on the assumption that a black revolution is bound to fail, and thus that the revolutionaries will not initiate their first-strike capability. As will be shown, the revolutionaries' decision to initiate a first strike against the armed forces is not deterred or based on the armed forces' second-strike capability, but rather may be based on the assumption of a third-strike capability accruing to the revolutionaries as a consequence of the armed forces' successful execution of its second-strke capability.

In all previous cases involving the use of federal troops to quell racial disorders their stay has been rather brief. There is no instance of federal troops (as distinct from the federalized National Guard) being kept in an area for as long as National Guard troops stayed in Wilmington after the King murder— nine months. However, in connection with the type of violence already described, which can be expected to occur over a period of two to four weeks of "dark terror," it is not likely that the security of a city so beleaguered would be quickly turned back to the National Guard or the local police. On the contrary, the likelihood is much higher for a protracted occupation of a city by federal troops in the event of planned terror.

Protracted occupation produces the first condition for a physical confrontation between the armed forces and the city's black population. After the lights and telephones were out it would be totally unwise for the general in command to allow things to operate except under his direction. After dark, people would not be permitted even to go to a nearby store for a loaf of bread. Maintaining security means population control, and consider how long it would take if every car and every person had to be searched before they were allowed to enter the inner city. Such security precautions can be made to work, but they neither eliminate the social friction they produce nor enable a highly interdependent society to work efficiently and productively. The decline in productivity in one sector of the economy produces bottlenecks, which in turn cause further shortages and signal the need to institute rationing of essential goods and services, and the shortages would hit the black community first. Theoretically, the federal troops would handle the rationing of available essentials on a share-and-share-alike basis among all citizens, but it would be especially difficult because of the resentment and fear the white community can be expected to feel toward the black community after the nights of terror and darkness. If blacks attempted to leave the inner city, either just to get away or to go to white neighborhoods to buy the things they needed which were unavailable in the ghetto, they would probably be met with hostility and closed stores. Even the most nonrevolutionary black is certain to take what action he deems necessary for his and his family's survival at that point. Patience runs out in a hurry when one's survival is at stake.

In such a situation, to prevent any possible white-black co-operation the black revolutionaries can count on the emergence of the paranoid, militant, anti-black right-wing paramilitary organizations as an active disruptive force. Most of these white extremists are just waiting for the chance to don their "white hats," pick up their weapons, and "kill some niggers" to put them in their place and teach them a lesson. Anyone who engages a paranoid right-winger in conversation comes away thinking the man cannot possibly be serious, but this group cannot be discounted if the black revolution goes beyond the state of "nights of darkness and terror" because their fear of blacks is likely to erupt in violence directed against innocent blacks. Once this occurs, the moment of truth is at hand for the armed forces.

Historically, all successful revolutions have been "won" at the point when the establishment's security forces chose not to shoot their countrymen. In the French Revolution when Louis XVI's palace guards threw down their rifles in the defense of the Bastille it was only a matter of months before the rest of the French Army melted away; in the Russian Revolution when the czar's elite guard units failed to shoot the members of the contending revolutionary factions attacking the Imperial Palace, the czar's government ceased to exist; in the Chinese Revolution when the Nationalist armies began to defect to the Communist side, Chiang Kai-shek and his government were through— although in all these cases there was much more fighting before all the centers of the old order's resistance and authority were finally destroyed.

In the American case, although it is not properly called a revolution, a similar situation is more responsible for American independence from England than is commonly supposed. Initially the situation involved Lord Amherst, the commander in chief of all of England's armed forces, who refused to take command in the field in America, although, inconsistently, he retained his title of commander in chief. According to G. O. Trevelyan, after Lord Amherst's refusal, Lord Howe went to America halfheartedly, salving his conscience by promising himself that he would do everything in his power to bring about a peace.[*]

Other, less important officers refused to go at all, in spite of the probable damage to their careers. In the spring of 1775 the Earl of Effingham was ordered to America with his regiment and repudiated his orders. He explained his refusal in the House of Lords, and it is worth repeating because it illustrated the problem with which a soldier is faced in a revolutionary situation. He said, "When the duties of a soldier and a citizen become inconsistent, I shall always think myself obliged to sink the character of the soldier in that of the citizen, till such time as those duties shall again, by the malice of our real enemies, become untied."[†] Six months later a similar view was expressed by one of Englands most famous war heroes, Lord Conway: "There is a great difference between a foreign war, where the whole community is involved, and a domestic war on points of civil contention, where the community is divided. In the first case no officer ought to call in question the justice of his country; but in the latter a military man, before he draws his sword against his fellow-subjects, ought to ask himself whether the cause was just or no."[**]

[*] G. O. Trevelyan, *The American Revolution* (New York: McKay, 1964), Vol. III, p. 202.

[†] *Ibid.*, p. 207.

[**] *Ibid.*, p. 208.

Such views had their effect. The English Army had to resort to Hessians, who were less than happy in their assignment, and although it took George Washington and his band of 6,000 to 30,000 ill-equipped misfits several years to bring Cornwallis to surrender in 1781, the issue was never really in doubt.* The point is that the theory of the impassive military instrument is most vulnerable in a revolution, where countryman is opposed to countryman.

But in our scenario, the armed forces' vulnerability to the revolutionary dilemma does not rest only on the fact that "soldiers are citizens like the rest of us," but also on the fact that many of those who are expected to put down a racially based disorder are themselves black and are considered to be different from "the rest of us."

This is not meant to allude to a potential for black mutiny in our nation's armed forces. Without exception, each of the military services has a racial problem, but their leadership is working on the problem. Not everyone in the military hierarchy is color-blind, but racism is not practiced as a matter of course in the United States armed forces. Certainly there is discrimination against blacks in the military, but in the past twenty years the armed services have been able to convince a large number of black Americans that "qualification" was not a restrictive word and that along with the necessity for qualification, which could be acquired, there was the corresponding access to positions of responsibility. Many blacks in the service are still skeptical about qualification and access, but nevertheless there has been a

---

* Few Americans are aware, by the way, that Negroes have fought in every war in which this nation has ever engaged. Ironically, the official policy (until this century) has been to keep Negroes out of the military and then to relent as the need for manpower became critical. George Washington set the pattern during the Revolutionary War, ordering his army not to enlist "any deserter from the ministerial army, nor any stroller, Negro or vagabond or persons suspected of being an enemy to the liberty of America." Washington may have set the pattern of institutional racism, but he had to change his orders when the British, promising freedom for black slaves, began enlisting them in Dunmore's Ethiopian Regiment. By the war's end, 5,000 of the 30,000 soldiers who fought the British were black. It is interesting to consider the prospect of the Daughters of the American Revolution being turned into a "black protest" organization if all those black Americans who are eligible to claim a revolutionary heritage were to join that ultra-segregationist society.

gradual increase of blacks in greater positions of responsibility throughout the armed forces.* The military has met the Supreme Court's injunction to proceed with the "greatest possible haste," and it is unfair to say otherwise. But after one acknowledges the military's past performance and continuing efforts to solve their internal racial problems, the revolutionary issue still remains.

Military leaders are not able to change the external conditions of racial imbalance and prejudice in our society, and that is part of the difficulty. When the black serviceman compares his status while in the service to his and others' status as civilians, and when he is met with bias in the towns surrounding his duty station, the very fact of being treated as a man in the service heightens his awareness of the gulf between fact and promise in American society. Nor can the military leadership alter the fact that between 38 and 40 per cent of those men in the Army and Marines who are nonrated (privates and privates first class) and who are further designated as Infantry soldiers happen to be black, and that is another part of the difficulty. Conspiracy has played no part in this. The black recruit, through no fault of his own, often lacks the educational achievements to qualify for the more sophisticated military assignments and schools, and consequently the great bulk of the black recruits end up as foot soldiers. Thus, as a result, the armed forces' real capacity to deal with a black revolution is affected by the presence of thir-

---

* Pentagon statistics show that blacks in the armed forces number more than 320,000, or about 9.4 per cent of the overall strength. In the Army, black soldiers account for some 11.5 per cent of the total. While black privates and privates first class range from 12.4 to 13 per cent, black sergeants first class come to 20.6 per cent and master sergeants to 15.7 per cent, showing a concentration of blacks in the two highest enlisted grades. The growing amount of qualification and access is also reflected in the statistics of the officer corps, which ten years ago was almost all white: in 1969 among Army officers there was one black general, 42 full colonels (.7 per cent of the total), 620 lieutenant colonels (3.7 per cent), 1,302 majors (5.5 per cent), 1,322 captains (3.7 per cent), 1,219 first lieutenants (2.9 per cent), and 616 second lieutenants (2.3 per cent). The Army has the largest number of black Americans of the military services, with approximately 167,599. This compares with 32,934 (4.5 per cent) for the Marine Corps and 78,789 (8.9 per cent) for the Air Force. Black officers in the Navy total 373 (.4 per cent), while in the Marine Corps they come to 231 (.9 per cent), and there are some 2,417 officers (1.8 per cent) in the Air Force.

ty-eight to forty black "rifle toters" in every hundred men who might be called upon to shoot and kill Americans in the line of duty.

How black troops would react to such orders is not entirely predictable, but on the basis of the actions of some forty black Vietnam veterans who were members of an elite Army airborne division and who requested (quite properly, and with dignity) to be excused from potential anti-riot duty in connection with President Johnson's orders to occupy Chicago at the time of the Democratic convention in 1968, one may conclude that black servicemen are not automatically prepared to use their killing talents against Americans, black or white. Furthermore, one may also conclude that the reluctance of black troops to engage in "hard" riot duty—that is, to shoot back and shoot to kill—probably correlates directly with the troops' length of service. Truly professional soldiers such as those in the French Foreign Legion are men without a country and do not bother to hate their opponents; however, it would be naïve to assume that this kind of detached attitude characterizes the typical drafted black infantry soldier. Thus we have a substantial number of black troops who may either respond to orders; respond to their consciences as did the French, Russian, and Chinese soldiers who refused to fire on their countrymen; or even, faced with paranoid anti-black right-wing groups, choose to lend their firepower to the revolutionary blacks.

No one knows the answers to these questions, but it is certainly in the interest of the black revolutionaries to make sure that the black troops consider them, because the revolutionaries know that once the troops refuse to respond to orders, the success of the revolution is assured, even if order is subsequently re-established. When black soldiers refuse, under direct orders, to shoot black men and women, even the most reluctant black citizen will be radicalized. From that moment on, the white establishment can no longer count on the black soldier, and to stay in power one must be sure of his subordinates.

This problem is further complicated by the fact that in the past two years there has been a stepped-up recruiting/agitation effort by the black activists and revolutionaries directed at black servicemen stationed in the United States. Former associates of mine have told me that the weekends on military bases from coast to coast are characterized by the presence of "soul brothers" who attempt to recruit and propagandize black servicemen. And if the government had been doing anything to provide a meaningful program for the 80,000 black combat veterans who return to civilian life each year we would probably have many fewer youthful potential black revolutionaries; but by mid-1969 there were more than 250,000 of these veterans who had been returned to civilian life without much more than a desultory "See you around."

It is in the interest of the black revolutionaries to force a confrontation either between federal troops and the black masses or between blacks and the paramilitary white right-wingers, which, in turn, would present the federal troops with the choice of firing on the whites, the blacks, or both. Each of these responses serve the black revolutionary equally well, and if the troops fail to fire at all, the establishment's third line of defense has been breached because it can no longer be considered sufficiently reliable by those in authority. Reliable troops can, of course, be found who under forceful leadership would be willing to shoot black and white alike and who would see the rioters and revolutionaries as mad dogs who must be exterminated. However, the success of federal troops who would be willing to use their firepower to put down a massive racial confrontation or a major intraracial disorder is illusory, because such action would only signal the end of the next-to-last act.

One might think that a scenario for a black revolution would end in an Armageddon type of grand-finale shoot-out, but this is not the case. As we have indicated, if the revolutionaries are to succeed they must eventually recruit radicalized black college students, and all the acts of terror and espionage and the engagement of more and more of the establishment's internal-security forces are designed to radicalize the black community, particularly the students. Because the last act of the revolution will consist of more of the guerrilla type of terror we have already described, on a larger scale, not only in major metropolitan centers but in smaller cities and towns, the revolutionaries will need enough persons with appropriate skills and ability to direct these widespread operations.

The imponderable in this entire process is whether it actually will motivate the black students to join the revolution. Massive reprisals almost certainly will provide the revolutionaries with recruits, but not necessarily those with the ability to lead. Thus even if the first phase of the revolution is successful, we are still not sure how the black students will react—with a whimper or a snarl. Perhaps they can be bought off or somehow neutralized by white society, but they are more likely to be radicalized if they are subjected to nondiscriminatory counterrevolutionary measures and then to join the black revolutionaries and take leading roles in the succeeding phases.

The epilogue question—or, more properly, the prologue question—to our black-revolution scenario cannot be answered with complete certainty—that is, are there really blacks in this country who are dedicated to undertaking such a venture? I am convinced that there are. Other societies, to their ultimate sorrow, ignored the revolutionary voices that openly announced their intentions. Those societies' leaders assumed that revolutionary rhetoric was just that—rhetoric. However, in the countries where revolution succeeded, the rhetoric preceded the act and was in fact part of the revolutionary process. Today we have a document called the Black Manifesto, adopted by the National Black Economic Development Conference on April 26, 1969, that may eventually become as famous as Karl Marx's Communist Manifestor, proclaimed in 1848. It clearly calls for a black revolution. A few of the pertinent paragraphs from the introduction follow (for the complete text, see Appendix A):

It is the power of the United States Government, this racist imperialist government, that is choking the life of all the people around the world. . . .

We live inside the U.S., which is the most barbaric country in the world, and we have a chance to help bring this government down.

Time is short and we do not have much time, and it is time we stop mincing words. Caution is fine, but no oppressed people ever gained their liberation until they were ready to fight, to use whatever means necessary, including the use of force and power of the gun to bring down the colonizer. . . .

We are the Vanguard Force. . . . We have suffered the most from racism and exploitation, cultural degradation and lack of political power. It follows from the laws of revolution that the most oppressed will make the revolution. . . .

But while we talk of revolution, which will be an armed confrontation and long years of sustained guerrilla warfare inside this country, we must also talk of the type of world we want to live in. We must commit ourselves to a society where the total means of production are taken from the rich and placed into the hands of the state for the welfare of all the people. . . .

Let us deal with some arguments that we should share power with whites. We say that there must be a revolutionary black Vanguard and that white people in this country must be willing to accept black leadership. . . . Only an armed, well-disciplined black-controlled government can insure the stamping out of racism in this country. . . .

We say, think in terms of total control of the U.S. Prepare ourselves to seize state power. . . .

The meaning of these quotes from the Black Manifesto is very clear, and there are other equally extreme statements being made by black activist leaders. Maybe we should take them more seriously than we are now inclined to.

There is one last argument the reader should consider before he makes his final judgment on whether he believes a black revolution can really happen here. This is a variation on Descartes' "gamble with God," wherein Descartes, who was a scientist, defended his belief in God (life after death) on the basis that to do so was not mystical but rational. To wit: if God did exist, by accepting God's existence—and inferentially His power —Descartes assured for himself, at no cost, eternal life; and, on the other hand, if God did not exist, then the erroneous belief was beneficial because it enabled Descartes to live a better, more peaceful and productive life. We can and should conceive of a black revolution in the same way. If we acknowledge and accept the potential for a black revolution, then we will be moved to take the hard but necessary steps to remove the underlying causes for it; and if the potential is not as real as it seems to be, then the actions we take to prevent it are those that we should have taken anyway to enable all citizens to live better, more peaceful and productive lives.

My own epilogue to this scenario is this: I have not gone into the tactics to stop a black revolution once it is underway because, as a matter of personal conviction, I believe that to use what talents I may possess to preserve our society's leadership if it refuses to act to *prevent* a black revolution is not in my own self-interest. If I, my family, and my friends perish as the result of such an attitude, so be it. It is better to die with one's dream intact than to live with another's nightmare.

SEVEN

Some Suggestions for "Counterrevolutionary" Social Action

THE PROBLEMS of race and race-related issues can no longer be left to the dictates of a system of national priorities determined by America's institutional power elites, which, armed with government authority, are largely unresponsive to public need and insulated from any significant criticism or reform. To persist in our entrenched ways is to invite disaster. There must be changes which will halt the increasing radicalization among our college students (particularly our black students); we must not let their potential for helping us find solutions become a potential for helping carry out a violent black revolution.

The only way to create the climate in which the changes suggested in this chapter can take place—a climate that will encourage reform rather than revolution—is to convince everyone, from the seemingly helpless individual citizen to the "power brokers," that we must act not from some abstract humanitarian principle but out of simple self-interest. If we don't, in the not-so-distant future our short-sightedness will bring us face to face with uncontrollable disorder. Short-term selfishness and apathy must give way to long-term selfishness, the kind of selfishness that makes each of us want to live in an orderly, truly free democratic society, simply because any other kind may destroy us all.

The gap between challenge and fulfillment is great, and we need all the help we can get to close it. We need the strength and vitality of the black community, particularly its college students, but we won't get it if we continue our piecemeal, stopgap programs full of grandiose promises followed by ineffectual action, or none at all. There is at present a feeling of helplessness and alienation that must be overcome, and to erase it there must be a commitment to innovative, realistic change by a broad-based elite made up of government leaders, the thousands of disturbed and devoted people who work in government, the millions of concerned and increasingly fearful citizens, and the young—those who are impatient with the status quo and feel that no real efforts are now being made to cope with our problems.

Without such a commitment, the actions suggested here—which are offered only as first steps, not as the full answer to our racial difficulties—will not be carried out, nor will any others. If the institutional power structures do not become more responsive to reason, logic, and practicality of such programs, the black revolution will proceed as planned.

Basically there are two aspects of our racial problem that we must deal with: the aspect of necessity and the social aspect. Necessity has caused revolution when the physical conditions of life deteriorated so far that the masses literally had nothing to lose by attacking the existing regime. Perhaps America has so far been spared a revolt based on necessity because in the past we have an abundance of land in relation to the size of our population, which made it possible for us to supply our basic needs and gave us new areas to settle—a "safety valve" which enabled our citizens to break away from unsatisfactory social conditions. However, today—in spite of a continuing increase in intraregional population shifts—there are no more open frontiers waiting to be settled by Americans. Most importantly, there is no way for black Americans to escape physically from their current environments. In large measure, the black American must live and die where he is today, in what must seem like islands of want surrounded by a sea of plenty, however polluted that sea of plenty may be.

Poverty and inequality in housing, employment, and education create a precondition for revolution because the black American believes—rightly or wrongly—that the American system has the ability to eliminate these inequities, and although he has been repeatedly told that they will be eliminated, they have not been. Patience has worn thin as a result of rising expectations in the face of continued frustration with the long-unattended ills of poor housing, lack of jobs, and inferior education. Each of these problems *can* be solved, but only after we stop the endless phase of "problem definition" and do the things required to remove the barriers to positive action.

Housing / One of the principal barriers to the improvement of ghetto housing is the fact that ownership of deteriorating tenements is very profitable because of a perversion in the law which was originally devised to encourage timely replacement of such capital items as apartment buildings. The slums represent a successful business venture in that there is an expanding ghetto population with a fixed—and, in most cities, a declining —supply of inner-city residential housing. This situation, together with depreciation laws for newly purchased but not necessarily new capital assets, enables landlords to use the law to block needed reconstruction of the inner cities and to make what must be considered inordinate profits. An example will explain how this process worked.

Landlord A buys a tenement with fifteen rental units at a purchase price of $200,000 with a down payment of $20,000 (10 per cent) and a government-insured mortgage of $180,000. He sets the average rent per unit at approximately $160 a month a month to produce an annual net rental income of $27,000 for the fifteen units, a figure in keeping with the national average of local taxes and amounts spent on rental-property maintenance of buildings with more than two rental units in inner-city areas and of rentals for this type of property. Out of his net income one might expect the landlord to pay some income taxes, but because he is also able to charge off the depreciation of his tenement against his current net income, he rarely does.

We can assume that the tenement is at least fifty years old (more than 70 per cent of all inner-city residential dwellings are more than fifty years old), and thus the landlord can declare the remaining life of his tenement to be, say, ten years and adopt a double-declining-digit method to gain the maximum amount of depreciation in the shortest period of time. That is, in the first year the depreciation allowed is equal to 20 per cent of the property's purchase price (10 per cent times 2 times $200,000, or $40,000), and in the second year it is 18 per cent of the property's remaining value (9 per cent times 2 times $160,000, or $28,-800). At the end of two years, or even after the first year, the owner is in a most desirable position to resell his investment, perhaps to a friend, associate, or relative; it is not uncommon to find a ghetto tenement changing hands as many as six times in ten years in order to take advantage of the depreciation gimmick.

Now let us assume that the property is sold for the same price—$200,000—to Landlord B, who also has been able to get a similarly insured government mortgage (since there is no shortage of tenants for slum housing, the government loan and the rental income are all but guaranteed). The new purchaser starts the depreciation process all over again. The original owner— who can and often does become the "third" owner after another two years—is able, under current laws, to net up to $68,000 as a tax-free return on his original down payment of $20,000, either by starting the process over again with another tenement, perhaps bought from Landlord B, or by charging the rest of the unused depreciation ($68,000 on a net income of $54,000 in a two-year period) off against other income. (This is not usually thought of as a tax loophole, but it works out that way.) A profit of $68,000 on a $20,000 two-year investment is handsome enough to keep the nation's slums in business, but, in addition, every dollar the landlord does not spend on repairs in the two years he owns the property represents 100 per cent tax-free profit as long as his rental income does not exceed the allowable depreciation charge, which explains why slumlords are so reluctant to repair, rehabilitate, or renovate their property.

Thus, the law actually promotes the very ends it was designed to prevent—that is, the continued existence of over-age, inferior housing. Landlords are able to profit at the expense of the poor and in the process worsen already intolerable living conditions. Tax equity, if nothing else, demands an end to this cycle of preferential treatment for those who exploit both black and white poor. The simplest solution is to amend the federal tax laws to disallow depreciation for a rental-housing unit more than forty years old while allowing the provision of the capital gains/losses to stand. This would force the slumlord, who often pays no taxes, to pay his fair share and would also lower the price of slum dwellings so that they could more easily be replaced. Taking the profit out of slumlordism will not by itself solve our ghetto housing problem, but as long as this condition exists, there is no reason to suppose anything of any substance will be done.

A second barrier to decent housing is the unwillingness of the building-trade unions to enter the twentieth century. Former Illinois Senator Paul Douglas, in his extensive study of the nation's housing ills conducted for the National Commission on Urban Problems, points out the impossibility of building the estimated required 26 million units of new housing in the next ten years as long as the jumble of special-interest building codes and material and labor-utilization restrictions are allowed to continue. There is no need to restate Senator Douglas' findings; they are well known and have not been effectively challenged. But even though the report details the reasons for change, it is not likely to be adopted unless drastic preliminary steps are taken.

There is no lack of new technology to solve our problems; there *is* a lack of leadership at the local, state, and federal level willing to rip down the barriers to action. What I am going to suggest may sound radical, but it represents the "how" in solving the national housing problem that primarily stems from local government inertia—antiquated building codes drawn up in response to trade union pressures. The federal government must bypass local government in Washington, D.C., in dealing with the housing problem there, and in the process create public pressure for the same kind of vigorous action in other cities.

Local, state, and federal governments are authorized to exercise the right of eminent domain for school and road construction. However, in Washington the federal government has the added authority to use eminent domain to acquire land for any purpose considered to be in the public interest or to promote the general welfare. Further, the Congress can either exercise directly, or pass to the executive branch, the authority to set aside or replace any and all of the existing building codes, conditions of work, etc. in the District of Columbia. This represents a great deal of potential power which can be used to break the nation's housing logjam. That is, the Congress and/or the executive branch can, without any additional authority, exercise the right of eminent domain to condemn every slum in the District of Columbia, buy the land at a price they determine to be fair, and inaugurate a program of urban renewal that calls on every possible phase of technology in order to build a truly model city. The program would not be based on outmoded building codes and restrictive labor practices designed to raise costs and provide featherbed jobs for trade union members, but on new, tested, effective techniques. It is possible to replace Washington's ghetto dwellings with low-cost public housing that is superior to that currently being erected as private luxury housing at a cost almost 25 per cent below that allowed or authorized for current public-housing units, and this housing would soon become a completely paying proposition.

Mass-produced quality housing is for sale today in several European countries, and it is cheap in comparison with current U.S. prices, simple to construct and maintain, and can be erected in an assembly-line manner that would eliminate most of the physical relocation associated with urban-renewal programs. If there are not enough persons in the trade unions who would be willing to work on a project that did not protect their special interests, there are nonunion construction workers in the black community available to do the job along with equally—if not more—competent electricians, plumbers, and engineers who happen to be members of the armed forces and who can be ordered to erect the new housing. We should remember that in World War II when we needed ships in a hurry, "Rosie the Riveter" was successfully brought into shipbuilding, which was characterized by the most restrictive labor practices known anywhere in the United States at the time. The same can be done for housing.

But to do this means the President and Congress must grab the bull by the horns and say that the building codes and trade union restrictions are out and that the elimination of the ghetto in the capital is a matter of national security that requires immediate and drastic action. Although there are problems connected with such a method, none is beyond our capacity to solve, and the benefits far outweigh the disadvantages. A "new" Washington would be the goad to force local governments to follow Washington's example because who would be willing to continue to pay high prices for low-quality housing, public or private, when the black population in the nation's capital was able to get better quality housing at a substantially lower price?

Employment/No one can be overly sanguine about quickly providing meaningful jobs for everyone in the black community, because it will take time to completely bridge the education and training gap. But there are actions that can be taken now to ease the tensions in this area and provide the impetus for the necessary training. Here again, as in the case of housing, the barriers to action are more of an issue than the specific actions themselves. Since job discrimination against blacks is due less to their lack of educational achievement than to personal and institutitional racism which denies them access to employment regardless of their qualifications, the first step is to remove the limits on upward mobility now facing the black worker. This would in turn open up jobs for less-qualified blacks at the bottom of the education ladder who are now unable to work because of the competition from overqualified blacks who are forced to take jobs below their ability. Two areas affecting black underemployment are especially crucial—the trade or craft unions and corporations which enjoy a high degree of market power due to their concentration.

In the case of the trade unions there was a spate of racial unrest in late 1969 when various black coalitions in Chicago, Pittsburgh, and other cities attempted to shut down government construction projects where the trade unions had engaged in racially discriminatory admission and hiring practices.* The black

* Decent work for blacks is scarce, and they are no longer satisfied with the menial tasks assigned to them; whites who are already employed,

position was well taken, because, in spite of George Meany's protestations concerning the AFL-CIO's color-blind admission policies, the facts clearly show that it is fifty times more difficult for a black man to become a master plumber than it is for him to become an M.D. Past performance indicates that exhortations by the highest of our government officials to labor's conscience —let alone the voices of the black man who wants and is able to do the work—are ignored. What is called for is to require the labor unions to show cause why their hiring and admission practices are *not* discriminatory, and to punish them physically and financially if they are.

Organized labor must be placed under the provisions of both the Sherman and Clayton anti-trust acts, or, if necessary, these acts should be amended or an anti-trust law aimed specifically at labor should be passed. In the past thirty years organized labor has acquired the power to fix prices and engage in restraint of trade by controlling entry into their unions on other than justifiable causes. The requirement to "show cause" would mean that if less than 2 per cent of a union's members were black the union's leaders would have to prove there were *no* qualified blacks available for membership—and this could not be done because there are many. If any union, local or national, was found guilty of this type of discriminatory restraint of trade, cash penalties would be assessed, and its leaders might even find themselves behind bars, just as did some highly placed officials of General Electric for fixing prices of electric generators. Such action would produce howls of protest from organized labor, but labor has no right to immunity from the law, which so far has enabled unions to remain financially secure at the expense of others while contributing to society's hardships.

And if nonunion, basically white-collar jobs for blacks are

---

of course, want to protect their jobs. However, in the Douglas study already cited, it was clearly shown that if the goals of the Housing Act of 1968 were put into effect there would be a labor shortage in the building trades, and it would then be profitable for building trades to compete for the talent of the poor, both black and white. Unfortunately, the logic of increasing housing and decreasing racism simultaneously is insufficient to provoke positive action or, for that matter, to cause President Nixon and Secretary Romney to redeem their 1968 pledges about housing and opening up new jobs.

to be opened up in any real numbers the big corporations will also have to mend their ways. The conventional wisdom, aided and abetted by the National Alliance of Businessmen, an organization of blue-chip firms, is that the big corporations have the most enlightened hiring policies and respond most readily to pleas for equal employment. Nevertheless, it has been demonstrated that the bigger the company, the poorer its record in equal opportunity in white-collar and nonunionized employment. William G. Shepherd, the assistant to the head of the Anti-Trust Division of the Department of Justice in the Johnson Administration, writing in the Spring 1969 issue of the *Anti-Trust Bulletin,* said, "Open hiring of Negroes is found mainly in competitive industries, in some lesser-sized firms in concentrated industries, and in non-profit entities." He found a direct correlation between economic concentration or market power and discriminatory hiring practices. Furthermore, using Census Bureau data, which is generally not available to scholars, Shepherd evaluated fifty-one industry groups ranging from oils and autos to brokers and lawyers in nine major cities and found that there was no essential difference between hiring patterns of blacks for white-collar jobs in the North and the South. (Blue-collar hiring practices were not included because of possible bias due to union pressures and the existence of such industrial unions as the United Auto Workers.)

Shepherd's studies show that highly concentrated industries such as the airlines, where fewer than four firms control 100 per cent of the market on any given route, rank among the lowest in hiring Negroes for white-collar jobs. The same results were found in other highly concentrated industries such as utilities, law firms, and cigarette makers. The highest rate of Negro white-collar employment was found in highly competitive business—personal services, beauty parlors, clothing stores, restaurants, and the like. The analysis was duplicated for the employment of Negroes as officials, managers, and professionals (generally considered the main areas of employment for black college graduates) and the results were the same: the greater the concentration in the industry group the smaller the Negro share of the jobs.

These studies are cited in some detail because they are relevant to another fact of economic life, which is, as has been argued thoroughly by John Kenneth Galbraith in *The Industrial State,* that more than 80 per cent of the dollar value of American industrial production is carried out by firms which are not subject to market forces and are run by managers who are careful to remain insulated from those forces. Because these firms provide most of the white-collar jobs, and because their record in nondiscriminatory hiring is so poor, it is unrealistic to look to them (except for a few in highly competitive industries and the telephone company, which employs a large percentage of black clerks) to lead the attack on discriminatory hiring unless they are compelled to do so or unless a plan is devised that will make it easier for them to do so. In spite of the big corporations' public relations pitch on how much they are doing to fight discrimination and how a firm bent on maximizing profits will hire anyone available at the lowest possible rate, if they sought to increase their profits by lowering their labor costs through hiring blacks at the "lowest possible rate," they would probably be prosecuted by the Anti-Trust Division for unfair competition. Thus they are in a "damned if you don't and damned if you do" dilemma.

Well, then, can corporations be compelled to hire blacks, as we have suggested for the trade unions, with or without a fixed percentage or quota? They could be subjected to a vigorous anti-trust policy which, together with the actions of the regulatory commissions, might at least require the regulated airlines, railroads, and utilities to hire more blacks. But since the situation is different from that of the trade unions, where "qualification" is an arbitrary precondition for membership and where the labor force is a homogenous element with a fixed group-negotiated wage rate, such rulings would probably be very difficult to enforce.

But there *is* a way out of the dilemma: to reduce the normal work week from the current forty hours to thirty or thirty-two. Such a move, which would require legislative action, would automatically open up more jobs for blacks because to avoid overtime costs it would be mandatory to expand the work force in order to maintain the total amount of profit on a corporation's capital investment. And the urge to maintain one's profit is a powerful incentive. Others might argue that the only *real* solution is growth of the Gross National Product, which would create new jobs, but growth is too unpredictable a factor to rely upon to meet the immediate requirement of large numbers of jobs for blacks. Furthermore, although it has not been proved that there is a causal relationship between the GNP and the nation's economic development, there is definitely a connection between increased growth and reduction in the normal work period. Arguments that such a move would be inflationary are not valid because the corporate desire to maintain profits can be counted upon to produce new efficiencies in production, which are largely avoided at the present because of a desire to escape anti-trust prosecution for engaging in "unfair competition."

So, if our goal is to provide jobs for blacks as quickly as possible, then spreading the existing amount of work among more people through a reduction in the work week would be the most effective means; corporations would have to hire blacks because of the current shortage in the available white work force.

Education / The final major area of discontent in the black community is inferior education. In Chapter Three we discussed the concept of the black university, which would help solve the problem of higher education, but the question of primary and secondary education for black children is more complex because of the sheer size of the problem. There is practically no one, North or South, who does not feel that quality education for all children is a desirable goal, and it should be remembered that the black community is not permanently wedded to desegregation of schools as *the* way to improve their children's education. They are more concerned with how to raise the quality of education efficiently and quickly.

In addition to using teaching machines more widely to help in teaching basic education skills and in remedial work, as suggested in Chapter Three, we must also consider the quality of the teacher in the urban ghetto schools and in the predominantly black schools throughout the South. It should be remembered that black teachers who are themselves the products of inferior ghetto education or a separate-but-unequal school system are not as well prepared, in general, as their white counterparts. Not only that, but both black and white teachers in ghetto schools are facing problems that teachers in middle-class schools are not called upon to face, to deal with situations and students that they have probably not been trained to deal with. This is not meant to denigrate the efforts of the teachers in black schools, for as a group they have tried hard, but they simply do not have the necessary background and training to teach in to-day's schools.

Therefore the black students' teachers should be required to go back to school themselves to learn to teach the new and ex-panded disciplines as well as how to teach the old ones more ef-ficiently, making use of modern technology. In the short run—the next seven to ten years—this means that the existing supply of teachers in predominantly black schools is going to have to be employed more intensively so that those who most urgently need upgrading will be able to further their own edu-cation during a year of special courses, and as they return to the classroom the better-qualified teachers will leave to receive ad-ditional training until all are brought fully up to the necessary standards.

These "re-education" programs must not rely on the con-ventional "teachers' college" approach, which is largely out-moded in relation to today's educational needs, but on the most advanced educational theories and on the concepts of industry leaders who have developed a full systems approach to the problem of incorporating new techniques and disciplines and who can be very valuable in helping to retrain our teachers. The costs of this program should be borne mostly by the federal government, as school boards dependent on a tax base for their upkeep cannot afford to pay for it on their own, nor should they have to. Closing the gap between black and white education is a national problem and as such it is the federal government's re-sponsibility to see that such a program is undertaken as soon as possible and not to let the costs get in the way.

This plan will not eliminate the goal of desegregation when and where it will work, nor does it mean that such serious ques-tions as community control of schools and the overbureau-cratization of school boards should be overlooked. But the re-education of teachers can be going on while these other issues are being settled, for the quality of our teachers must be improved regardless of whether education is integrated, locally controlled, or its administration is in dispute.

In 1968 President Johnson established Project Transition to provide training to men leaving the military without marketable civilian skills. Unfortunately, under the Nixon Administration, Project Transition has been allowed to languish and extremely little has been done in this area. Secretary of Defense Melvin Laird established a Domestic Action Council in the spring of 1969 to administer Project Transition and other military programs designed to bring some of the military's talents and expertise to bear on our current domestic problems, but these efforts have been more verbal than real.

An example of the kind of program that might be helpful is one conducted in 1969 by the Staten Island Community College of the City University of New York. Their College Discovery Program provided remedial training to twenty combat veterans, all of whom were either black or members of other minority groups, at Fort Dix, New Jersey, during their last few months of their military service. College authorities provided the veterans with remedial training in fundamental knowledge skills and a stipend following successful completion of the training course. This was important because it is very difficult for a black soldier who has been out of school for several years or who has completed high school on the basis of a General Education Test to attend college without some support from the institution.

A greatly expanded College Discovery Program among black servicemen who have completed their Vietnam service and are marking time until their return to civilian life would have two advantages in working against a black revolution. First, providing remedial education and helping them enroll in colleges in their home states would supply a "countervailing presence" on the nation's campuses to that of the rule-or-ruin student protesters who do not really seem to want an education. It seems somewhat perverse for colleges to concentrate so heavily on "high-risk" black high school students and to ignore those who, although older, have shown their worth to the nation and their sense of responsibility for their actions. Second, providing a worthwhile alternative to the mind-wasting make-work tasks for the noncareer combat veterans might help lower interracial tensions in stateside military bases. But assistance to the black veteran is valuable in its own right, of course, as well as being a means to lessen the possibility of interracial violence in the armed forces and on campuses.

If such a program is to be inaugurated on any meaningful scale we must have vigorous leadership, which seems to be almost totally lacking in the federal government and the institutions of higher education. A comment made by one of the Fort Dix soldiers upon completion of the training course for the Staten Island Community College's program should be taken to heart by our leaders: "We're not going to tell you how grateful we are. We're going to benefit from what you have given us and try not to let you down." There is considerable promise in that statement, and the fact that 250,000 black combat veterans have already left military service with next to nothing done for them to prevent their subsequent radicalization should reinforce it. They would be real assets to a black revolution because they have already learned how to fight a guerrilla war.

The Social Aspect / The other half of our racial problem is concerned with relationships between whites and blacks, either singly or in groups. These, too, should be based upon an objective appreciation of one's own rational, long-term self-interest rather than merely on vague concepts of good will and brotherhood for the sake of brotherhood. Many of our relationships, personal and institutional, are complicated because we persist in seeing each other as homogeneous groups, or as individuals who are part of such groups, without being aware of individual differences and qualities. This is the sort of attitude that not only produces racist behavior, when the view is a negative one, but hampers effective social action if it is a benevolent, "let's help everyone" view.

To take group relationships first, we must discard our worn-out humanistic concepts of helping everyone who needs it, which results in helping no one effectively because there simply aren't enough resources—human or monetary—to do the job thoroughly for everyone. Instead, however difficult the choices are, however "heartless" it may seem, we must learn to differentiate among those groups who can be helped and those who can't—or at least not without an inordinate amount of money spent for what may be very little return. We must begin to concentrate our efforts and our dollars more selectively on those who can be helped—college students, young children, teachers, the underemployed—and not get caught in the trap of stopgap welfare and piecemeal rehabilitative programs for those who are least likely to benefit from it.

Perhaps a hypothetical example might make this clearer. The director of an institution with responsibilities for social welfare has $1,000 and is expected to spend it in the most beneficial way. He has before him a six-year-old who has demonstrated a great deal of potential that requires immediate cultivation if it is to be realized and a sixteen-year-old who has demonstrated almost total social disorientation in the form of criminal behavior. The director has been advised by competent, objective authorities that the cost of bringing the six-year-old up to a self-sustaining take-off point is $1,000 and that if this opportunity is missed the child will probably never achieve his full potential. He has also been told that $1,000 will only begin therapy for the sixteen-year-old and that there is only a 50-50 chance of rehabilitating him even if much more money is spent in his behalf. What would be the wisest decision in this case in terms of both human potential and society's long-term benefit?

There is no denial of the worth of human life in this kind of institutional-categorization process, because to sustain a more productive, useful life rather than sacrifice it in order to try to sustain a less productive life is consistent with the appreciation of the worth of a human being and its uniqueness. It might be contended that it is inhuman to ascribe greater worth to one individual than to another and to the categories in which they fall, but to do otherwise—and end up helping no one—will eventually destroy us all. Furthermore, the choice between objectively based competing claims for man's capacity to help his fellow man denies the universal need for superiority over other human beings and enables institutions to operate on a more supportable basis.

It is becoming apparent that, since public institutions have taken over social responsibility without making the hard choices among competing claims, individual whites are growing more hostile toward all blacks and are losing faith in the very principle of social responsibility. This intensifies the effects of institutional racism and worsens the conditions that institutional social responsibility was supposed to alleviate. Because the overwhelming majority of whites are aware of blacks only through services provided by institutions (and at times of racial unrest), it is vital that institutions' actions be based on a rational appreciation, and support, of ends and means. In recent years white responses to blacks—and vice versa—have become more negative because so much institutional performance has produced a discriminatory effect without gain. As long as welfare, for example, wasn't too costly and the recipients were tractable and grateful, individual whites did not have to have an attitude toward blacks—that is, they could avoid assuming an attitude. However, welfare has become more costly and the recipients are demanding more and are no longer quietly grateful, and both black and white attitudes are hardening and institutional racism is growing rather than diminishing.

As a specific example of how the institution of welfare could be changed to provide truly constructive help rather than temporary aid, we should consider the following proposal. Instead of providing day-care centers (which may or may not have value to preschool children) for mothers who can't go out to work because they must stay with their children, we could make arrangements for the children to live apart from their mothers in a kibbutz type of environment in which the children's development is not left to chance or to a mother who may not be able to meet the child's needs. If the children are seen as objects of value to be developed and nurtured by the entire society rather than as just another aspect of the "Negro problem" or simply as "love objects" the choice becomes less difficult to make. No one suggests that an Israeli mother who places her children in a kibbutz loves them less; the opposite is true, because she knows that in order for her children to survive and achieve their fullest potential it is essential to do what is best for them. A similar arrangement here would not have to be mandatory, for mothers would welcome a program that treated their children as unique, valuable human beings rather than as mere pawns in the welfare battles. And whereas day-care centers may release mothers to get jobs, a kibbutz type of program would not only release mothers but also build useful future citizens by providing a constructive environment for the ghetto's poorest children.

The basic thing to be said about personal interracial relationships is that both parties must try to approach each other with neither preconceived notions that members of another race are the embodiments of all the stereotyped racial characteristics we've heard about throughout our lives nor with an attitude of indiscriminate good will and a feeling that "all men are just alike." There are differences—but they are differences of personality, intelligence, family background, education, and environment as much as they are of race. There are similarities—but it is self-defeating to see any other person as just another undifferentiated lump of mankind and not to acknowledge his specific attributes.

This may seem to be an obvious observation, but nevertheless many of us—of both races—never have a chance to meet each other as individuals, as thinking beings, and not in some standardized role. Most often we are aware of each other only through the relatively sensational news events we see on TV or read about in newspapers and magazines, and thus rarely do we have the opportunity to put our preconceived notions to the test. And we all have preconceived notions, whether we are aware of them or not, and we do not come to personal interracial encounters with a clean slate as far as racial attitudes are concerned.

I went to Howard University to find out what the black college students were actually saying about the world around them. To pay my way for the opportunity to listen to them I taught them some of the principles of economics, but I received more than I gave, because the students paid me a hundred times over through what they were willing to teach me, about themselves and about myself. We talked a great deal about interpersonal relationships between the races, and they were natural, honest, and understanding, as they were throughout our talks. When we were discussing how one would know when he had kicked racism out of his personal relationships, one of the students said, "When you can freely say, without any feeling of guilt, 'You stupid so and so' and leave off the unnecessary adjective 'black'—you're there!"

That is a simple but profound truth, although it may be harder and harder for us to attain it if we become even more polarized and our relationships become even more fragile as the specter of racial violence takes more definite shape. This does not have to happen, if we listen to the black college students and learn from what they have to say. It does not have to happen if we look at ourselves and our own long-term self-interest and act—decisively—in that interest. No single action taken by an individual or a group, publicly or privately, is going to eliminate racism and its side effects or the potential for revolution, but each action *not* taken to chip away at racism threatens our nation's future.

There are some hopeful signs. Management groups have been formed to help black businesses and corporations are establishing black companies; college students are doing tutorial work in the ghettos; military personnel are participating in community-action projects in their off-duty hours; private citizens are volunteering to act as unpaid professional and technical advisers to community colleges and to remedial-training programs in technical schools. These and many other actions are being taken, but we need to do much more, and it cannot be left to chance or to government initiative. To eliminate racism, make use of the full potential of the black minority, and avoid a black revolution—to bring about meaningful, positive, peaceful social change—is a task for all Americans.

APPENDIX A

The Black Manifesto

FOLLOWING IS the text of the "Black Manifesto as presented, with an introduction, by James Forman and adopted by the National Black Economic Development Conference in Detroit on April 26, 1969. It was addressed to "the white Christian churches and the Jewish synagogues in the United States of America and all other racist institutions."

INTRODUCTION

We have come from all over the country, burning with anger and despair not only with the miserable economic plight of our people, but fully aware that the racism on which the Western World was built dominates our lives. There can be no separation of the problems of racism from the problems of our economic political, and cultural degradation. To any black man, this is clear.

But there are still some of our people who are clinging to the rhetoric of the Negro and we must separate ourselves from those Negroes who go around the country promoting all types of schemes for Black Capitalism.

Ironically, some of the most militant Black Nationalists, as they call themselves, have been the first to jump on the bandwagon of black capitalism.

They are pimps, Black Power pimps and fraudulent leaders, and the people must be educated to understand that any black man or Negro who is advocating a perpetuation of capitalism inside the United States is in fact seeking not only his ultimate destruction and death, but is contributing to the continuous exploitation of black people all around the world. For it is the power of the United States Government, this racist, imperialist government, that is choking the life of all people around the world.

We are an African people. We sit back and watch the Jews in this country make Israel a powerful conservative state in the Middle

East, but we are not concerned actively about the plight of our brothers in Africa. We are the most advanced technological group of black people in the world, and there are many skills that could be offered to Africa.

At the same time, it must be publicly stated that many African leaders are in disarray themselves, having been duped into following the lines as laid out by the Western Imperialist government.

Africans themselves succumbed to and are victims of the power of the United States. For instance, during the summer of 1967, as the representatives of SNCC, Howard Moore and I traveled extensively in Tanzania and Zambia. We talked to high, very high, governmental officials. We told them there were many black people in the United States who were willing to come and work in Africa.

All these government officials, who were part of the leadership in their respective governments, said they wanted us to send as many skilled people that we could contact. But this program never came into fruition and we do not know the exact reasons, for I assure you that we talked and were committed to making this a successful program.

It is our guess that the United States put the squeeze on these countries, for such a program directed by SNCC would have been too dangerous to the international prestige of the U.S. It is also possible that some of the wild statements by some black leader frightened the Africans.

In Africa today, there is a great suspicion of black people in this country. This is a correct suspicion since most of the Negroes who have left the States for work in Africa usually work for the Central Intelligence Agency (CIA) or the State Department. But the respect for us as a people continues to mount and the day will come when we can return to our homeland as brothers and sisters.

But we should not think of going back to Africa today, for we are located in a strategic position. We live inside the U.S., which is the most barbaric country in the world, and we have a chance to help bring this government down.

Time is short and we do not have much time, and it is time we stop mincing words. Caution is fine, but no oppressed people ever gained their liberation until they were ready to fight, to use whatever means necessary, including the use of force and power of the gun to bring down the colonizer.

We have heard that rhetoric, but we have not heard the rhetoric which says that black people in this country must understand that we are the Vanguard Force. We shall liberate all the people in the U.S.

and we will be instrumental in the liberation of colored people the world around.

We must understand this point very clearly so that we are not trapped into diversionary and reactionary movements. Any class analysis of the U.S. shows very clearly that black people are the most oppressed group of people inside the United States. We have suffered the most from racism and exploitation, cultural degradation and lack of political power. It follows from the laws of revolution that the most oppressed will make the revolution, but we are not talking about just making the revolution.

All the parties on the left who consider themselves revolutionary will say that blacks are the Vanguard, but we are saying that not only are we the Vanguard, but we must assume leadership, total control and we must exercise the humanity which is inherent in us.

We are the most humane people within the U.S. We have suffered and we understand suffering. Our hearts go out to the Vietnamese for we know what it is to suffer under the domination of racist America. Our hearts, our soul and all the compassion we can mount goes out to our brothers in Africa, Santo Domingo, Latin America and Asia who are being tricked by the power structure of the U.S. which is dominating the world today. These ruthless, barbaric men have systematically tried to kill all people and organizations opposed to its imperialism.

We no longer can just get by with the use of the word capitalism to describe the U.S., for it is an imperial power, sending money, missionaries and the army throughout the world to protect this government and the few rich whites who control it. General Motors and all the major auto industries are in operation in South Africa, and yet the white-dominated leadership of the United Auto Workers sees no relationship to the exploitation of black people in South Africa and the exploitation of black people in the U.S.

If they understand it, they certainly do not put it into practice, which is the actual test. We as black people must be concerned with the total conditions of all black people in the world.

But while we talk of revolution, which will be an armed confrontation and long years of sustained guerrilla warfare inside this country, we must also talk of the type of world we want to live in. We must commit ourselves to a society where the total means of production are taken from the rich and placed into the hands of the state for the welfare of all the people. This is what we mean when we say total control.

And we mean that black people who have suffered the most from exploitation and racism must move to protect their black interest by assuming leadership inside of the United States of everything that exists. The time has passed when we are second in command and the white boy stands on top.

This is especially true of the Welfare Agencies in this country, but it is not enough to say that a black man is on top. He must be committed to building the new society, to taking the wealth away from the rich people such as General Motors, Ford, Chrysler, the Du-Ponts, the Rockefellers, the Mellons, and all the other rich white exploiters and racists who run this world.

Where do we begin? We have already started. We started the moment we were brought to this country. In fact, we started on the shores of Africa, for we have always resisted attempts to make us slaves and now we must resist the attempt to make us capitalists. It is the financial interest of the U. S. to make us capitalist, for this will be the same line as that of integration into the mainstream of American life.

Therefore, brothers and sisters, there is no need to fall into the trap that we have to get an ideology. We *have* an ideology. Our fight is against racism, capitalism and imperialism and we are dedicated to building a socialist society inside the United States where the total means of production and distribution are in the hands of the United States and that must be led by black people people, by revolutionary blacks who are concerned about the total humanity of this world.

And, therefore, we obviously are different from some of those who seek a black nation in the United States, for there is no way for that nation to be viable if in fact the United States remains in the hands of white racists.

Then, too, let us deal with some arguments that we should share power with whites. We say there must be a revolutionary black Vanguard and that white people in this country must be willing to accept black leadership, for that is the only protection that black people have to protect ourselves from racism rising again in this country.

Racism in the U.S. is so pervasive in the mentality of whites that only an armed, well-disciplined, black-controlled government can insure the stamping out of racism in this country. And that is why we plead with black people not to be talking about a few crumbs, a few thousand dollars for this cooperative, or a thousand dollars which splits black people into fighting over the dollar. That is the intention of the government.

We say: think in terms of total control of the U.S. Prepare ourselves to seize state power. Do not hedge, for time is short and all around the world the forces of liberation are directing their attacks against the U.S.

It is a powerful country, but that power is not greater than that of black people. We work the chief industries in this country and we could cripple the economy while the brothers fought guerrilla warfare in the streets. This will take some long-range planning, but whether it happens in a thousand years is of no consequence. It cannot happen unless we start.

How then is all of this related to this conference?

First of all, this conference is called by a set of religious people, Christians, who have been involved in the exploitation and rape of black people since the country was founded.

The missionary goes hand in hand with the power of the states. We must begin seizing power wherever we are and we must say to the planners of this conference that you are no longer in charge. We the people who have assembled here thank you for getting us here, but we are going to assume power over the conference and determine from this moment on the direction in which we want it to go.

We are not saying that the conference was planned badly. The staff of the conference has worked hard—have done a magnificent job in bringing all of us together and we must include them in the new membership which must surface from this point on. The conference is now the property of the people who are assembled here.

This we proclaim as fact and not rhetoric and there are demands that we are going to make and we insist that the planners of this conference help us implement them.

We maintain we have the revolutionary right to do this. We have the same rights, if you will, as the Christians had in going into Africa and raping our Motherland and bringing us away from our continent of peace and into this hostile and alien environment where we have been living in perpetual warfare since 1619.

Our seizure of power at this conference is based on a program and our program is contained in the following manifesto:

BLACK MANIFESTO

We the black people assembled in Detroit, Michigan, for the National Black Economic Development Conference are fully aware that we have been forced to come together because racist white America has exploited our resources, our minds, our bodies, our labor. For centuries we have been forced to live as colonized people inside the United States, victimized by the most vicious, racist system in the world. We have helped to build the most industrial country in the world.

We are therefore demanding of the white Christian churches and Jewish synagogues which are part and parcel of the system of capitalism, that they begin to pay reparations to black people in this country.

We are demanding $500,000,000 from the Christian white churches and the Jewish synagogues. This total comes to 15 dollars per nigger. This is a low estimate, for we maintain there are probably more than 30,000,000 black people in this country. Fifteen dollars a nigger is not a large sum of money and we know that the churches and synagogues have a tremendous wealth and its membership, white America, has profited, and still exploits black people.

We are not unaware that the exploitation of colored peoples around the world is aided and abetted by the white Christian churches and synagogues. This demand for $500,000,000 is not an idle resolution or empty words. Fifteen dollars for every black brother and sister in the United States is only a beginning of the reparations due us as people who have been exploited and degraded, brutalized, killed and persecuted.

Underneath all of this exploitation, the racism of this country had produced a psychological effect upon us that we are beginning to shake off. We are no longer afraid to demand our full rights as a people in this decadent society.

We are demanding $500,000,000 to be spent in the following way:

1. We call for the establishment of a Southern land bank to help our brothers and sisters who have to leave their land because of racist pressure for people who want to establish co-operative farms, but who have no funds. We have seen too many farmers evicted from their homes because they have dared to defy the white racism of this country. We need money for land. We must fight for massive sums of money for this Southern Land Bank. We call for $200,000,000 to implement this program.

2. We call for the establishment of four major publishing and printing industries in the United States to be funded with $10,-000,000 each. These publishing houses are to be located in Detroit, Atlanta, Los Angeles, and New York. They will help to generate capital for further cooperative investments in the black community, provide jobs and an alternative to the white-dominated and controlled printing field.

3. We call for the establishment of four of the most advanced scientific and futuristic audio-visual networks to be located in Detroit,

Chicago, Cleveland and Washington D.C. These TV networks will provide an alternative to the racist propaganda that fills the current television networks. Each of these TV networks will be funded by $10,000,000 each.

4. We call for a research skills center which will provide research on the problems of black people. This center must be funded with no less than $30,000,000.

5. We call for the establishment of a training center for the teaching of skills in community organization, photography, movie making, television making and repair, radio building and repair and all other skills needed in communication. This training center shall be funded with no less than $10,000,000.

6. We recognize the role of the National Welfare Rights Organization and we intend to work with them. We call for $10,000,000 to assist in the organization of welfare recipients. We want to organize the welfare workers in this country so that they may demand more money from the government and better administration of the welfare system of this country.

7. We call for $20,000,000 to establish a National Black Labor Strike and Defense Fund. This is necessary for the protection of black workers and their families who are fighting racist working conditions in this country.

8. We call for the establishment of the International Black Appeal (IBA). This International Black Appeal will be funded with no less than $20,000,000. The IBA is charged with producing more capital for the establishment of cooperative businesses in the United States and in Africa, our Motherland. The International Black Appeal is one of the most important demands that we are making, for we know that it can generate and raise funds throughout the United States and help our African brothers. The IBA is charged with three functions and shall be headed by James Forman:

(a) Raising money for the program of the national Black Economic Development Conference.

(b) The development of cooperatives in African countries and support of African Liberation movements.

(c) Establishment of a Black Anti-Defamation League which will protect our African image.

9. We call for the establishment of a Black University to be funded with $130,000,000 to be located in the South. Negotiations are presently under way with a Southern University.

10. We demand that IFCO allocate all unused funds in the planning budget to implement the demands of this conference.

In order to win our demands we are aware that we will have to have massive support, therefore:

1. We call upon all black people throughout the United States to consider themselves as members of the National Black Economic Development Conference and to act in unity to help force the racist white Christian churches and Jewish synagogues to implement these demands.

2. We call upon all the concerned black people across the country to contact black workers, black women, black students and the black unemployed, community groups, welfare organizations, teacher organizations, church leaders and organizations explaining how these demands are vital to the black community of the U.S. Pressure by whatever means necessary should be applied to the white power structure of the racist white Christian churches and Jewish synagogues. All black people should act boldly in confronting and demanding this modest reparation of 15 dollars per black man.

3. Delegates and members of the National Black Economic Development Conference are urged to call press conferences in the cities and to attempt to get as many black organizations as possible to support the demands of the conference. The quick use of the press in the local areas will heighten the tension and these demands must be attempted to be won in a short period of time, although we are prepared for protracted and long range struggle.

4. We call for the total disruption of selected church-sponsored agencies operating anywhere in the U.S. and the world. Black workers, black women, black students and the black unemployed are encouraged to seize the offices, telephones and printing apparatus of all church-sponsored agencies and to hold these in trusteeship until our demands are met.

5. We call upon all delegates and members of the National Black Economic Development Conference to stage sit-in demonstrations at selected black and white churches. This is not to be interpreted as a continuation of the sit-in movement of the early sixties, but we know that active confrontation inside white churches is possible and will strengthen the possibility of meeting our demands. Such confrontation can take the form of reading the Black Manifesto instead of a sermon or passing it out to church members. The principle of self-defense should be applied if attacked.

6. On May 4, 1969, or a date thereafter, depending upon local conditions, we call upon black people to commence the disruption of the racist churches and synagogues throughout the United States.

7. We call upon IFCO to serve as a central staff to coordinate

the mandate of the conference and to reproduce and distribute en mass literature, leaflets, news items, press releases and other material.

8. We call upon all delegates to find within the white community those forces which will work under the leadership of blacks to implement those demands by whatever means necessary. By taking such actions, white Americans will demonstrate concretely that they are willing to fight the white-skin privilege and the white supremacy and racism which has forced us black people to make these demands.

9. We call upon all white Christians and Jews to practice patience, tolerance, understanding and nonviolence as they have encouraged, advised and demanded that we as black people should do throughout our entire enforced slavery in the United States. The true test of their faith and belief in the Cross and the words of the prophets will certainly be put to a test as we seek legitimate and extremely modest reparations for our role in developing the industrial base of the Western world through our slave labor. But we are no longer slaves, we are men, and women, proud of our African heritage, determined to have our dignity.

10. We are so proud of our African heritage and realize concretely that our struggle is not only to make revolution in the United States, but to protect our brothers and sisters in Africa and to help them rid themselves of racism, capitalism, and imperialism by whatever means necessary, including armed struggle. We are and must be willing to fight the defamation of our African image wherever it rears its ugly head. We are therefore charging the Steering Committee to create a Black Anti-Defamation League to be funded by money raised from the International Black Appeal.

11. We fully recognize that revolution in the United States and Africa, our Motherland, is more than a one-dimensional operation. It will require the total integration of the political, economic and military components and therefore we call upon all our brothers and sisters who have acquired training and expertise in the fields of engineering, electronics and research, community organization, physics, biology, chemistry, mathematics, medicine, military science and warfare to assist the National Black Economic Development Conference in the implementation of its program.

12. To implement these demands we must have a fearless leadership. We must have a leadership which is willing to battle the church establishment to implement these demands.

To win our demands we will have to declare war on the white Christian churches and synagogues, and this means we may have to fight the total government structure of this country. Let no one here think that these demands will be met by our merely stating them. For the sake of the churches and synagogues, we hope that they have the wisdom to understand that these demands are modest and reasonable.

But if the white Christians and Jews are not willing to meet our demands through peace and good will, then we declare war and we are prepared to fight by whatever means necessary. We are, therefore, proposing the election of the following Steering Committee:

Lucius Walker, Renny Freeman, Luke Tripp, Howard Fuller, James Forman, John Watson, Dan Aldridge, John Williams, Ken Cockrel, Chuck Wooten, Fannie Lou Hamer, Julian Bond, Mark Comfort, Earl Allen, Robert Browne, Vincent Harding, Mike Hamlin, Len Holt, Peter Bernard, Michael Wright, Muhammed Kenyatta, Mel Jackson, Howard Moore, Harold Holmes.

Brothers and sisters, we no longer are shuffling our feet and scratching our heads. We are tall, black and proud.

And we say to the white Christian churches and Jewish synagogues, to the government of this country and to all the white racist imperialists who compose it, there is only one thing left that you can do to further degrade black people and that is to kill us. But we have been dying too long for this country. We have died in every war. We are dying in Vietnam today fighting the wrong enemy.

The new black man wants to live, and to live means that we must not become static or merely believe in self-defense. We must boldly go out and attack the white Western world at its power centers.

The white Christian churches are another form of government in this country and they are used by the government of this country to exploit the people of Latin America, Asia and Africa, but the day is soon coming to an end. Therefore, brothers and sisters, the demands we make upon the white Christian churches and the Jewish synagogues are small demands.

They represent 15 dollars per black person in these United States. We can legitimately demand this from the church power structure. We must demand more from the United States Government.

But to win our demands from the church which is linked up with the United States Government, we must not forget that it will ultimately be by force and power that we will win.

We are not threatening the churches. We are saying that we know the churches came with the military might of the colonizers and have been sustained by the military might of the colonizers.

Hence, if the churches in colonial territories were established by military might, we know deep within our hearts that we must be prepared to use force to get our demands. We are not saying that this is the road we want to take. It is not, but let us be very clear that we are not opposed to force and we are not opposed to violence.

We were captured in Africa by violence. We were kept in bondage and political servitude and forced to work as slaves by the military machinery and the Christian churches working hand in hand.

We recognize that in issuing this manifesto we must prepare for a long-range educational campaign in all communities of this country, but we know that the Christian churches have contributed to our oppression in white America.

We do not intend to abuse our black brothers and sisters in black churches who have uncritically accepted Christianity. We want them to understand how the racist white Christian church with its hypocritical declarations and doctrines of brotherhood has abused our trust and faith.

An attack on the religious beliefs of black people is not our major objective, even though we know that we were not Christians when we were brought to this country, but that Christianity was used to help enslave us. Our objective in issuing this Manifesto is to force the racist white Christian church to begin the payment of reparations which are due to all black people, not only by the Church but also by private business and the U.S. government.

We see this focus on the Christian church as an effort around which all black people can unite.

Our demands are negotiable, but they cannot be minimized, they can only be increased and the Church is asked to come up with larger sums of money than we are asking. Our slogans are:

All roads must lead to revolution.

Unite with whoever you can unite.

Neutralize wherever possible.

Fight our enemies relentlessly.

Victory to the people.

Life and good health to mankind.

Resistance to domination by the White Christian churches and the Jewish synagogues.

Revolutionary black power.

We shall win without a doubt.

APPENDIX B

Strategies for Dealing with Student Campus Takeovers

ONE ISSUE that did not fit comfortably into the context of this book but that is of interest is that of how college and university administrators should respond when confronted with student seizure, violence, and destruction. This matter is of interest not only in itself but relates to the radicalization of black students in that the more wisely university administrators deal with student uprisings the less likelihood there is of violent confrontations between students and off-campus security forces. Such confrontations, as we have seen, tend to fit into potential revolutionaries' plans because many previously uncommitted students are often radicalized as a result.

The possible responses range from the "police bust" ordered by President Pusey at Harvard, the use of National Guard troops and police as called for by Acting President Hayakawa at San Francisco State, and court injunctions, as employed at Howard University, to the passive-resistance technique of President Levi at the University of Chicago and the yet-to-be-tried tactic used by Robert E. Lee at Washington & Lee University in the 1870s when he posted a notice saying that if demonstrations and protests were not stopped immediately he would close the school.

Each of these tactics has some merit, but those involving the police, the National Guard, or court injunctions are generally the least effective. Force *per se* is only successful in an insurrectional situation if it can be applied selectively quickly, and efficiently against a specific target, and this presents a problem to police or troops in a campus uprising because they are not familiar with the campus and are unable to identify and fix the real targets. Unfortunately, most educators only understand force and its application in an abstract sense. Thus, when there is "overkill" because of an inability to apply force selectively and quickly, they assume an attitude of moral repugnance toward the use of force, which is hypocritical since they were the ones to call for the outside help to solve their problems with the student protesters in the first place. Governor Reagan, who does not claim to be an educator, was far more honest with student militants when he said that regardless of the consequences he would apply all or part of the force at his disposal to oppose them if they violated any criminal statutes. It is better to tell a protester that he will be shot than to say—*after* he is shot—"I'm sorry—that hurt me more than it did you."

In both the Harvard and San Francisco State cases, where there was no communication between the students and the administration, siege tactics were called for instead of a police rush. This might have made martyrs out of some of the militants, but it would not have made radicals out of the uncommitted students, and the uncommitted are the key to lasting success in any insurrectional action. On the other hand, President Levi at Chicago employed siege tactics without siege forces and was able to maintain communication with the students throughout the confrontation. He said that even if the militants burned the campus down he would not interpose the police, as an independent force, between himself and the striking students, which reflected his willingness to run substantial risks and his recognition that if the militants *did* burn the school down the uncommitted students would reject radical tactics as the means to achieve reform in the university.

Furthermore, although the use of a court injunction by Howard University's authorities to break a student sit-in succeeded in ending the strike, it was of little long-term value because it, like the use of police and troops, shifted authority for maintaining control over the university from an internal to an external organization. To disavow, after the fact, the actions taken by an external organization to restore order on a campus is useless because once the authority to act is passed to an external group, the school administration has no control over the means used. The lesson, then, to be drawn from the use of outside forces to quell student disturbances is that once a university administration abdicates its responsibility and authority to outside forces there is no way, short of mass resignations of those in charge, to resume control and direction over the university in the future. Such administrators only delude themselves and their trustees if they think they are really back in charge after the disturbance has been put down.

The tactic of student violence must be met with a countertactic, not a counterattack. President Levi's use of a Gandhian type of passive resistance may be successful if the routine of classes can be maintained; however, if student occupation, seizure, and violence is so widespread that classes are called off, even on a limited basis, the expedient of closing the school for an indefinite period is more effective. Certainly both these solutions beg the issue of criminal trespass, but to treat protest in isolation, as a violation of criminal law, is not effective. Political protest cannot be resolved in terms of criminality, although this seems to be the only method acceptable to some defenders of the status quo.

There is, however, a method that can be used to keep protest from escalating into violence, and it is really quite simple. It is to apply what I call the "comply with fraud" principle.

A typical student protest entails the presentation by an articulate minority of demands—either specific or nonspecific—for reforms in the operations of a university. In essence, the minority arrogates unto itself the role of spokesman for the entire student body of which it is but a small part, and this—regardless of the merit of their demands— is essentially nondemocratic. The basis of the comply-with-fraud principle is to accept the articulate minority's demands as if they had been made by *all* the students and then subject them to binding democratic ratification by the entire student body. The minority cannot object, if this is done openly and publicly. If the demands are not fraudulent they will be supported by students and faculty; if they are fraudulent the best way to expose them is to have the student body, in whose name they are made, do so.

As an example, if a demand is made to drop grades, then the grades will be dropped, but only after a campuswide plebiscite whose results will be binding on all students based on a simple majority-vote decision. It is very likely that a student body faced with the prospect of the university providing potential employers only with a statement to the effect that "John Jones was in residence at this university from September 1969 to June 1973" will mobilize its own counterprotest. However, if after debate and discussion the students vote to support the demand for no grades, it will indicate that they are willing to defer the evaluation of their performance to some element outside the academic environment. At present, universities make the initial evaluation of students for employers by assigning grades, but there is no immutable reason for this, and it may not be a necessary or worthwhile function. The issue of "fraud or not fraud" goes to the heart of the matter of student protest because when they call for "no grades" the students may be saying that to be of real value education must not attempt to serve two masters—the business world and the students. But the point is that it would be interesting and not permanently damaging to higher education to see if the students were willing to forgo their partial ticket of admission to the "outside" world on principle, or if they would prefer to receive compensation for their studies in some externally acceptable form.

Using the comply-with-fraud principle would enable an established authority to provide a positive test of the protesters' intentions and the extent of their actual power and support as well as the value of new ideas by treating demands for change as hypotheses to be subjected to verification or rejection. It would take some courage for university administrators to apply this tactic, because they might be forced to comply with decisions that call for sweeping reform, but to be afraid to take that chance is to invite continued disruption and polarization.

SELECTED BIBLIOGRAPHY

Acton, Lord. *Lectures on the French Revolution* (1910). New York, 1959.

Adams, John. *Works* (10 vols.). Boston, 1851.

Allport, G. W. *The Nature of Prejudice*. Cambridge, Mass., 1954.

Aptheker, Herbert, ed. *A Documentary History of the Negro People in the United States* (2 vols.). New York, 1951.

———. *Negro Slave Revolts*. New York, 1943.

Arendt, Hannah. *On Revolution*. New York, 1963.

———. *The Origins of Totalitarianism*. New York, 1958.

Bardolph, Richard. *The Negro Vanguard*. New York, 1943.

"Black Power and the White Radical," A Radical Newspaper of the Committee for Independent Political Action, October 21,1966.

Boggs, James. "Black Power: A Scientific Concept Whose Time Has Come," *Liberator*, May, 1967.

———. "Power! Black Power!" *Liberator*, January 1967.

Braden, Anne. "The SNCC Trends: Challenge to White America," *The Southern Patriot*, May 1966.

Breitman, George. "In Defense of Black Power," *International Socialist Review*, January-February 1967.

Brotz, Howard. *The Black Jews of Harlem: Negro Nationalism and the Dilemmas of Negro Leadership*. New York, 1964.

Carmichael, Stokely, and Charles V. Hamilton. *Black Power: The Politics of Liberation in America*. New York, 1967.

Chicago Commission on Race Relations. *The Negro in Chicago: A Study of Race Relations and a Race Riot*. Chicago, 1922.

Clark, Kenneth B. *Dark Ghetto: Dilemmas of Social Power*. New York, 1965.

Clausewitz, Karl von. *On War*. Washington, D.C., 1953.

Cleaver, Eldridge. *Soul on Ice*. New York, 1968.

Cromwell, John W. *The Early Convention Movement*. American Negro Academy, Occasional Papers No. 9, Washington, D.C., 1905.

Cruse, Harold. *The Crisis of the Negro Intellectual*. New York, 1967.

Delany, Martin R. *The Niger Valley Exploration Party*. New York, 1861.

Dollard, John. *Caste and Class in a Southern Town.* New York, 1949.

DuBois, W. E. B. *Black Reconstruction.* New York, 1935.

Drucker, Peter F. *The Age of Discontinuity.* New York, 1968.

Ellison, Ralph. *Invisible Man.* New York, 1947.

Essein-Udon, E. U. *Black Nationalism.* New York, 1964.

Fager, Charles E. *White Reflections on Black Power.* Grand Rapids, Mich., 1967.

Fanon, Frantz. *Black Skin, White Masks.* New York, 1967.

———. *The Wretched of the Earth.* New York, 1963.

Fiddick, Thomas C. "Black Power, Capitalism and Vietnam," *Liberation,* September 1966.

Franklin, John H. *From Slavery to Freedom.* New York, 1956.

Frazier, E. Franklin. *Black Bourgeoisie: The Rise of a New Middle Class in the United States.* Glencoe, Ill., 1957.

Friedberg, Bernard, William McCord, John Howard, and Edwin Harwood. *Life Styles in the Black Ghetto.* New York, 1969.

Garfinkel, Herbert. *When Negroes March.* Glencoe, Ill., 1959.

Gilbert, Ben W. *Ten Blocks from the White House: Anatomy of the Washington Riots, 1968.* New York, 1968.

Graham, Hugh Davis, and Ted Robert Gurr. *Violence in America: Historical and Comparative Perspectives.* New York, 1969.

Grant, Joanne, ed. *Black Protest.* Greenwich, Conn., 1968.

Gregory, Dick, with Robert Lipsyte. *Nigger: An Autobiography.* New York, 1964.

Grier, William H., and Price M. Cobbs. *Black Rage.* New York, 1968.

Grodzins, Morton. *The Loyal and the Disloyal: Social Boundaries of Patriotism and Treason.* Chicago, 1956.

———. *Americans Betrayed: Politics and the Japanese Evacuation.* Chicago, 1949.

Hare, Nathan. *The Black Anglo-Saxons.* New York, 1965.

———. "Behind the Black College Student Revolt," *Ebony,* August 1967.

Haywood, H. *Negro Liberation.* New York, 1948.

Hentoff, Nat. "Applying Black Power," *Evergreen Review,* December 1966.

Hernton, Calvin C. *Sex and Racism in America.* Garden City, N.Y., 1965.

Herskovits, Melville J. *The Myth of the Negro Past.* New York, 1941.

Holt, Len. *The Summer That Didn't End.* New York, 1965.

Hofstader, Richard. *The Paranoid Style in American Politics.* New York, 1965.

Jacobs, Paul. *Prelude to Riot: A View of Urban America from the Bottom.* New York, 1968.

James, Selwyn. *South of the Congo.* New York, 1943.

Jehlen, Alen. "Black Power and Political Strategy," *New Left Notes,* November 11, 1966.

Jones, LeRoi. *The System of Dante's Hell.* New York, 1965.

Janowitz, Morris. *Social Control of Escalated Riots.* Chicago, 1968.

Killens, John O. *Black Man's Burden.* New York, 1965.

Kozol, Jonathan. *Death at an Early Age.* Boston, 1967.

Lasswell, Harold D. *Politics, "Who Gets What When and How."* Cleveland, 1958.

Lemberg Center for the Study of Violence. *Riot Data Review.* Brandeis University, 1968.

Lenin, V. I. "State and Revolution" (1918), *Collected Works.* New York, 1932.

Lincoln, C. Eric. *The Black Muslims in America.* Boston, 1961.

Lomax, Louis E. *When the World Is Given: A Report on Elijah Muhammad, Malcolm X and the Black Muslim World.* Cleveland, 1963.

Malcolm X. *The Autobiography of Malcolm X.* New York, 1964.

Mannix, Danile P. *Black Cargoes.* New York, 1962.

Mao Tse-tung. *Works* (4 vols.). Peking, 1958.

Margolis, Richard J. "The Two Nations at Wesleyan University," *The New York Times Magazine,* January 18, 1970.

Marx Karl. *The Communist Manifesto* (1848). New York, Modern Library edition.

——. *Das Kapital* (1873). New York, Modern Library edition.

McNeill, Robert B. "Black Revolution: How Should Whites Respond?" *Together,* May 1967.

Meyer, F. S. "Negro Revolution: A New Phase," *National Review,* October 4, 1966.

Myrdal, Gunnar. *An American Dilemma* (2 vols.). New York, 1944.

Nelson, Truman. *The Torture of Mothers.* New York, 1965.

Newman, Richard. "The Black Power Revolution," *Boston University Graduate Journal,* Fall 1967.

Palmer, Robert R. *Twelve Who Ruled: The Year of Terror in the French Revolution.* Princeton, 1941.

Patterson, William. "Black Power, Blackmail, Backlash," *American Dialog,* November-December 1966.

Peck, James. "Black Racism," *Liberation,* October 1966.

Powledge, Fred. *Black Power, White Resistance: Notes on the New Civil War.* Cleveland, 1967.

Quarles, Benjamin. *The Negro in the American Revolution*. Chapel Hill, N.C., 1961.

Rabson, Grace Rubin. "Behavioral Science Versus Intelligence," *Wall Street Journal*, July 18, 1969.

Roberts, Gene. "Negro Nationalism: A Black Power Key," *The New York Times Magazine*, July 24, 1966.

Report of the National Advisory Commission on Civil Disorders. New York, 1968.

Sargent, S. S., and R. C. Williamson. *Social Psychology*. New York, 1958.

Schuyler, George S. "The Caucasian Problem," in *What the Negro Wants*. Edited by Rayford W. Logan. Chapel Hill, N.C., 1944.

———. "Negroes Speak Out Against Militants," *Christian Economics*, January 10, 1967.

Sheppard, Barry. "Black Power Attacked by Old Guard Leaders," *The Militant*, October 24, 1966.

Silberman, Charles. *Crisis in Black and White*. New York, 1964.

Staudenraus, P. J. *The African Colonization Movement, 1816–1865*. New York, 1961.

Thompson, Daniel C. *The Negro Leadership Class*. Englewood Cliffs, N.J., 1963.

Towne, Anthony. "Revolution and the Marks of Baptism," *Katallegete*, Summer 1967.

Tumin, Melvin M. *Desegregation: Resistance and Readiness*. Princeton, N.J., 1958.

Urban America, Inc., and the Urban Coalition. *One Year Later: An Assessment of the Nation's Response to the Crisis Described by the National Advisory Commission on Civil Disorders*. New York, 1969.

Waskow, Arthur I. *From Race Riot to Sit-In*. New York, 1966.

Walsh, Edmund A. *Total Power*. New York, 1948.

Williams, Robert F. *Negroes with Guns*. New York, 1962.

Wilson, C. E. "Black Power and the Myth of Black Racism," *Liberation*, September 1966.

Wilson, James Q. *Negro Politics: The Search for Leadership*. Glencoe, Ill., 1960.

———. *Varieties of Police Behavior*. Cambridge, Mass., 1968.

Wright, Nathan, Jr. *Black Power and Urban Unrest*. New York, 1967.

Providence
Public Library

To take a book from the Library without having it charged is an offense against the rights of other readers, and a violation of the rules of the Library and the laws of the State.

Examine this book carefully before taking it home. If found to be damaged or needing repairs, report it. Otherwise, you will be held responsible for its condition.

DEMCO